Union County's Black Soldiers and Sailors of the Civil War

Union County's Black Soldiers and Sailors of the Civil War

Ethel M. Washington

The History Press

Published by The History Press
Charleston, SC 29403
www.historypress.net

Front cover images: Courtesy Scotch Plains Historical Society, New York Public Library and the author.
Back cover image: Courtesy New York Public Library.

First published 2011
Manufactured in the United States
ISBN 978.1.59629.446.2

Library of Congress Cataloging-in-Publication Data

Washington, Ethel M.
Union County's Black soldiers and sailors of the Civil War / Ethel M. Washington.
p. cm.
Includes bibliographical references.
ISBN 978-1-59629-446-2
1. Union County (N. J.)--Genealogy. 2. African American soldiers--New Jersey--Union County--History--19th century--Registers. 3. African American sailors--New Jersey--Union County--History--19th century--Registers. 4. New Jersey--History--Civil War, 1861-1865--Registers. 5. United States--History--Civil War, 1861-1865--Registers. 6. New Jersey--History--Civil War, 1861-1865--Participation, African American. 7. United States--History--Civil War, 1861-1865--Participation, African American. I. Title.
F142.U5W38 2011
973.7'415--dc22
2011012910

Contents

Preface

April 12, 2011, marks the commemoration of the sesquicentennial of the Civil War. The impending 150th anniversary of the Civil War was the catalyst for a research and writing journey I embarked on seven years ago, culminating with this illustrated history of black soldiers and sailors of Union County, New Jersey, through photographs, documents, service records, personal letters and tombstone inscriptions. While the focus of this book is limited to this geographical area, it has relevancy at the state and national level.

History has shown that those who write the books are the ones who determine the legacies. So it is that this history is chronicled from a personal perspective and based on what I have learned during my seven years of research on the topic; what I intuit from my experiences as a black American growing up in the segregated South and reaching maturity in the "integrated" North; what scholars have and have not said; and what others have written.

On an ironic note, I have written this book in the spirit of Corporal Joseph T. Wilson (b. 1837), whose comrades proposed to him in 1882 "that the history of the American negro soldier should be written, that prosperity might have a fuller and more complete record of the deeds of the negro soldiers than had been given in the numerous already published histories of the conflicts in which they played so important a part." The unheralded Corporal Wilson who served honorably in Company G, Second Louisiana Native Guard (Second Colored Infantry), and Company K of the famed Fifty-fourth Massachusetts Infantry, felt it was his duty to accept the task proposed to him by his fellow soldiers. In 1888, Private Wilson published his 528-page book, *The Black Phalanx: A History of the Negro Soldiers of the United States in the Wars of 1775–1812, 1861–'65.*

In the preface to this prophetic work, Wilson wrote:

> *It seemed proper, also, that the memory of our forefathers should not be allowed to remain in longer obscurity; that it was fitting to recall* their *deeds of heroism, that all might know the sacrifices they made for the freedom their descendants were so long denied from enjoying…My aim has been to write in the spirit which impelled the soldiers to go forth to battle, and to reverse the accounts given in the popular histories which ascribe to the generals and colonels who commanded, instead of the soldiers who did the fighting, victory or defeat.*[1]

This book is dedicated to the ancestors, Joseph T. Wilson and all of his comrades of African descent, including those with ties to Union County, New Jersey, as a result of birth, residency, burial site or enlistment in one or more of the regiments organized in the county.

Acknowledgements

This research project would not have come to fruition had it not been for the support and outstanding contributions of the individuals, institutions and research sources acknowledged below. A special thanks to my local copy editors, friend and Central State University of Ohio classmate Ann Troupe Thornhill and Rex Nobles of Hunter College in New York City. A special debt of gratitude is owed to the New Jersey Historical Commission for a generous fiscal year 2009 Special Project Grant award, without which the publication of this book would not have been possible.

Accessible Archives On-line Database (Tom Nagy, chief operating officer)
Historical Data Systems, America Civil War Research Database
Library of Congress
Mother Bethel A.M.E. Church, Richard Allen Archives, Philadelphia, Pennsylvania
National Park Service's Civil War Soldiers and Sailors System Database
New Jersey Historical Society
New Jersey State Archives, Department of State
New York Historical Society
New York Public Library
New York State Archives Cultural Education Center, Albany, New York
New York State Military Museum and Veterans Research Center, Saratoga Springs, New York
U.S. Army Military History Institute, Carlisle, Pennsylvania

William S. Stryker's Record of Officers and Men of New Jersey in the Civil War, 1861–1865
Ron Becker, Rutgers University Special Collections, Alexander Library
Beatrice Bernzott, Linden Historical Society
Richard T. Koles, Union County Historical Society
Jessie Levine, Historical Society of Plainfield
Salvatore Mione, Union County Office of Veteran Affairs
Joanne M. Nestor, Principal Photographer, New Jersey State Archives
Harold Scheidegger, Evergreen Cemetery, Hillside, New Jersey

Chapter 1

Black Life in Union County: 1857–66

Union County was created by an act of the New Jersey legislature on March 19, 1857, taking effect on April 13, 1857. Formed from the southern portion of Essex County, the original municipalities created by the time of the outbreak of the Civil War in 1861 included Elizabeth, Rahway, Union, Westfield, Plainfield, New Providence, Linden, a portion of Springfield and Clark. At the time, the majority of blacks resided in Elizabeth, Rahway, Plainfield and Westfield, respectively.

According to the census of 1860, Union County had a total free aggregate population of 27,780. Out of this number, 381 were native-born black men, 418 women; 20 native-born mulattoes (mixed race) men, 40 women; 1 foreign-born black man, 3 black women; and 2 foreign-born mulatto women. The total number of citizens in Union County of African ancestry at the coming of the war was 865.[2]

Despite the passage of the Gradual Emancipation Act of 1804 by the New Jersey state legislature, slavery was not formally outlawed until the passage of a second law in 1846. This law created an apprenticeship system but still failed to fully emancipate all those covered by it. All black children born after its passage were declared free. Blacks who were already slaves became "apprentices" for life. It was not until the end of the Civil War in 1865 that the Thirteenth Amendment to the United States Constitution finally ended involuntary servitude in New Jersey.

Little attention has been given to former slaves from New Jersey that suited up as Union soldiers. In a letter to a friend, dated July 22, 1865, former slave

Horace Reed (b. 1857), a resident of Elizabeth, was born into slavery in Dinwiddie County, Virginia. WPA/ New Jersey Writers Project/ Photographs, ca. 1935–42. *Courtesy New Jersey State Archives.*

Slave quarters located on Grove Street in Elizabeth, WPA/New Jersey Writers Project/ Photographs, ca. 1935–42. *Courtesy New Jersey State Archives.*

and veteran Edward Slater of Rahway wrote, "I am enjoying a freedman's life very much indeed. I don't know how I stood being a slave so long do you but I rejoice to think that slavery is dead." Rahway-born George Jackson (1820–1899) was drafted into the war and then emancipated. Elizabeth resident Horace A. Reed (b. 1859) was born into slavery in Virginia. Slave quarters on Grove Street in Elizabeth, which remained standing until the 1930s, served as a constant reminder that slavery in the South, as well as the industrial North, was central to the causation of war.

The living environment of Union County blacks was clearly defined by the outbreak of the war and reflective of the political, economic and social climate of New Jersey, recently described as the "least Free-soil" in sentiment. Although all Union County blacks were "free" by 1860, they were precluded from any meaningful participation in mainstream social, economic and political activities that paralleled the lives of blacks throughout New Jersey during one of the nation's most disturbing chapters of history.

By 1861, Union County was well on its way to developing an industrial base and transportation infrastructure. The overall economic life of Union County was given a major boost with the outbreak of the Civil War. Carriage- and coach-making factories in Elizabeth and Rahway received large contracts from the United States government for wagons, ambulances, guns, saddles and shoes. J.A. Bannister of Elizabeth was awarded an order for 100,000 pairs of shoes for the growing army; John Urmston's Rahway Steam Hub Manufactory was contracted for its production of oak and elm hubs used for army wagons, ambulances and gun carriages. The Rutan Shipyards in Elizabeth's port was kept busy, repairing existing ships and building new ones for battle. Other Elizabeth factories experiencing the economic boost were John N. Burger and Sons, makers of boots; Elizabeth Manufacturing Company, iron castings; S.L. Moore and Sons, Foundry; Eugene Munsell and Company, Foundry; and Bowker Fertilizer Company.

The economic prospects for blacks remained dim despite the economic boost of the war. In 1860, 59.6 percent of Elizabeth's free black population of 301 found employment as common laborers, skilled craftsmen, painters, carpenters and blacksmiths; 16.9 percent were unskilled; and 15.7 percent were service workers. Peter Lee (1804–1902), a former slave, spent his life as a servant for the Stevens family of Hoboken, while Henry Schenck worked as a servant on the John Marsh estate in Scotch Plains.

Civil War veteran Elijah Pippenger (1825–1895) was the unpaid town crier of Rahway. An 1891 article by H.L. Moore offered this description of the

Above, left: Private Henry Shenck was a servant on the John Marsh estate on Park Avenue and Front Street, Scotch Plains. *Courtesy Scotch Plains Historical Society.*

Above, right: Private Elijah Pippenger (1825–1895) was a popular town crier in Rahway. *Courtesy Afro-American Research Library and Museum, Rahway.*

popular town crier: "Pippenger is not pedantic, but seems to delight in using big words, indulging sometimes in a regular fusillade to the astonishment of the illiterate and delectation of the erudite." For seventeen years, Pippenger worked for the editor of Rahway's *Union Democrat* as the "hand-power," or motor, for the production of the newspaper. He lost his job after being replaced with the newly invented modern press that was powered by steam.

Despite general poverty and lack of opportunity, a fragile black middle class emerged from Elizabeth, Rahway, Plainfield and Westfield families. Among those whose roots and accomplishments are traceable to the early 1800s are the families of Kinch, Tunison, Edgar, Randolph, Crowell, Marsh, Wyckoff and Cromwell. Peter H. Wyckoff (1820–1893) was a successful Plainfield broom maker whose net worth had risen to $3,800 by 1870. Civil War veteran George Randolph (1814–January 10, 1884) of Plainfield, a founding member of Mount Olive Baptist Church in Plainfield, reported a personal estate worth more than $3,000.

Daniel and Edmonia Edgar of Rahway built the first house on U.S. Highway 1, which was originally named Edgar Road. Ernest L. Brown was a successful Rahway caterer, earning enough to put his son, Joseph E. Brown

Above, left: John W. Cromwell (1846–?). The Cromwell family's roots in Union County are traceable to the early 1800s. *Courtesy New York Public Library.*

Above, right: Private Peter H. Wyckoff (1820–1893), a Plainfield broom maker, helped establish Mount Olive Baptist Church, Plainfield, in 1870. *Courtesy of the author.*

(b. February 7, 1888), through medical school. In 1862, Samuel Edgar, Anthony Jamison and Jacob Moore purchased property for the construction of Bethel/Ebenezer AME Church in Rahway.

Among the blacks receiving a formal education during this period are teachers William G. McKinney and Hiram Wyckoff and engineers Theodore Williams and James Vermeule of Elizabeth.

By the time of the war, a group of highly visible black church activists and abolitionists were on the scene and drew on their experiences as slaves and free people to illuminate the plight of blacks. Throughout the antebellum years, Union County blacks attended antislavery lectures and political speeches delivered by leaders from neighboring Newark and New York City. In many instances, messages were delivered from the pulpit of a church. Churches were effectively converted into bastions of the black American freedom/equality struggle.

The overwhelming majority of local black worshippers belonged to one of three denominations: Presbyterian, African Methodist Episcopal (AME) or Baptist. The earliest religious experiences on record were largely within the white Presbyterian churches where "negro pews" were used to separate white and black parishioners. They were identified on church membership rolls by the lower case "c," for colored.

Discriminatory practices within white churches led to the establishment of mission chapels and/or churches out of "mother" churches in both Elizabeth and Plainfield. Licensed in 1823 by the Presbytery of New Jersey to preach to other blacks, the Reverend William G. Pennington led the earliest black religious ceremonies of that denomination in Elizabeth. He provided both traditional religious guidance and political leadership to all blacks.

Twenty-six black members of the First Presbyterian Church of Elizabeth (Old First Church) withdrew their letters of membership between 1859 and 1860. This group, along with black worshippers from other churches, established an informal Colored Presbyterian Church, which thrived under the leadership of the Reverend Daniel H. Vandervere. In 1863, the Reverend Vandervere served as a trustee of the African Civilization Society, which encouraged self-reliance and self-government for blacks returning to Africa with the encouragement of the African Colonization Society. Members of the African Civilization Society made it clear in an 1864 supplement to its constitution that their organization was not designed to encourage general emigration but to aid blacks who were qualified and "suited" to promote the development of Christianity, morality, education, mechanical arts, agriculture, commerce and general improvement.

At the September 1859 church dedication ceremony, the Reverend Henry Highland Garnet (1815–1882), a leading member of the generation of blacks who led the abolition movement to political action, delivered the keynote sermon. The Reverend Garnet, ordained in 1843 in the Presbyterian church, devoted his life to the ministry. He was known for his oratorical powers and delivered a passionate sermon in which he encouraged and supported black efforts of self-improvement. The Colored Presbyterian Church's formal ties to the First Presbyterian Church, Elizabeth, were not severed until 1866. The mission officially incorporated itself as the Siloam Presbyterian Church, making it the third black Presbyterian church to be founded in New Jersey.

The First and Second Presbyterian Churches of Rahway, organized in 1741 and 1849 respectively, had a major impact on the lives of many Rahway blacks, including Amos Noe Freeman (1809-1893). He was pastor of Siloam Presbyterian Church, Brooklyn, born in Rahway, orphaned at an early age and raised within the Rahway Presbyterian Church. After briefly attending the old Rahway Academy built by a black Rahway citizen, Samuel Oliver, Freeman was sent to the African Free School in Manhattan, from which he graduated. He attended the Oneida Institute, near Rochester, New York. He never graduated but was ordained and installed in Portland, Maine, in 1841. The Reverend Freeman came to Brooklyn in 1852, and with the exception of three and a half years in Hartford, he occupied the pulpit of Siloam Presbyterian Church until 1885. He was twice appointed moderator for the Brooklyn Presbytery.

The Reverend Freeman returned to his hometown of Rahway for many speaking engagements. On March 26, 1834, he spoke at a meeting of the Anti-Colonization Society of the Free Colored Inhabitants of Rahway. An editor at a leading African American newspaper wrote, "Mr. Amos Freeman arose and addressed the meeting in a very appropriate and spirited manner."[3]

A known agent of the Underground Railroad during the mid-1850s, the Reverend Freeman helped Anna Maria Weems (b. 1840), a young girl fleeing southern slavery, by providing her shelter in his family home. He later disguised her as a boy and personally delivered her to freedom in Ontario, Canada.

In 1849, fifty-five members of Rahway's First Presbyterian Church, at their own request, were dismissed by the session to organize the Second Presbyterian Church. The surnames of black families listed on the original 1849 church membership roll, and later on Civil War regimental rosters, include Freeman, Crowell, Edgar, Oliver, Morse, Connett, Potter, Mulford, Randolph, Marsh, Vanderhoven, Noe and McKinney.

Segregation and discrimination in the majority churches spurred a movement for independent black churches in the north. Mother Bethel African Methodist Episcopal (AME) Church of Philadelphia, formed in 1816, is recognized as the genesis of this black religious movement. By the time of the Civil War, Bethel's reach had spread throughout the region. Its founding father and first elected bishop, the Reverend Richard Allen (1760–1831) of Philadelphia, had solidified a regional network of churches, including in Rahway and Elizabeth. Divided into four conferences, Elizabeth and Rahway were a part of the Philadelphia Conference.

Ana Maria Weems escaped slavery through the Underground Railroad with the assistance of Rahway-born Amos Noe Freeman. *Courtesy New York Public Library.*

In 1826, a small group of Rahway blacks established Ebenezer AME

Church, making it the third oldest of this denomination in New Jersey. From 1826 to 1829, members held their services in various homes and were supplied with a number of pastors who remained for a short time. In 1829, thirty or more families of "free persons of color" procured the church's current site on Central Avenue and erected its first building. The signers of the deed were Civil War veterans Samuel Edgar, Anthony Jamison and Jacob Moore. The Reverend Christopher Voorhies, the organizer, served as the church's first pastor. A new sanctuary, which originally carried the name of the Philadelphia mother church, Bethel Methodist Church, was built in 1862.

Seven of Ebenezer's supply pastors, all clerical descendents of the Reverend Allen, would go on to be elected bishops and community leaders, including Daniel A. Payne (1811–1893), James A. Shorter (1817–1887), Alexander W. Wayman (1821–1895), William Paul Quinn (1788–1873) and Jabez Pitt Campbell (1815–1891). The bishops regularly returned to Rahway and Elizabeth to provide religious guidance and sermons related to the black struggle for equality.

The Reverend Campbell, who was consecrated a bishop of the AME church in 1864, was the most radical of the bishops. In 1861, he questioned President Lincoln's commitment to the abolition of slavery and spoke out about the discriminatory practices toward black soldiers. By war's end, Bishop Campbell had taken on a more optimistic view about the future of blacks. In a sermon delivered at the end of the war in 1865, Bishop Campbell told an audience of over two hundred, "There is a future before us which will be very much modified, for weal or for woe, by our own conduct. Let us act worthy of our new and growing privileges."[4]

Elizabeth's oldest independent black church, Mount Teaman African Methodist Episcopal Church, began as a small congregation on Washington Street in the 1850s. It was formally organized in 1862. Under the direction of its first pastor, the Reverend Alfred Lawrence, an activist, would in 1872 attend the very first convention of black voters of New Jersey, where he composed and proposed the resolutions adopted during the one-day meeting. Mount Teaman provided religious guidance and a place for blacks to enjoy a myriad of rights as citizens. A forum was provided to express, without recrimination, political aspirations during the original "turbulent" '60s. The congregants of Mount Teaman benefitted from its close proximity to Newark, a center of black activism. Newark had been home to the abolitionist and Presbyterian minister Reverend Samuel E. Cornish, cofounder in 1827 of *Freedom's Journal*, the first African American newspaper.

African Methodist Episcopal Church bishops Payne, Shorter, Wayman, Quinn and Campbell were supply pastors at Ebenezer A.M.E. Church, Rahway. *Courtesy New York Public Library.*

African Methodist Episcopal bishop Jabez P. Campbell (1815–1891) questioned President Lincoln's commitment to the abolition of slavery. *Courtesy Mother Bethel A.M.E. Church, Richard Allen Archives.*

Union County black Baptist churches were all formally organized after the Civil War. Elizabeth's Shiloh Baptist Church, which was organized in 1879 by members who withdrew from Elizabeth's Fourth Baptist Church; Mount Olive Baptist Church, the oldest of Plainfield's Black congregations, withdrew from First Baptist Church and established itself in 1870; and Cranford's First Baptist Church was organized in 1887. Westfield's Bethel Baptist Church was organized in 1893 as the New York Avenue Baptist Church. Prior to their establishment, groups of black Baptist churches had their origins in majority white Baptist churches in their respective towns. The common thread among these churches is that, during the antebellum years, small groups of progressive blacks of the Baptist faith held religious gatherings in different places and helped establish the social fabric for many forms of social expressions.

In 1807, the state legislature of New Jersey restricted voting rights to white men, eliminating privileges that the state's 1776 constitution had extended to both blacks and women. Despite sustained black opposition to the 1807 restriction, New Jersey's 1844 constitution continued to limit the franchise to white men.

New Jersey was the only Northern state to vote against Abraham Lincoln in the presidential elections of both 1860 and 1864. The state's electorate divided between Republican Abraham Lincoln and Democrat Stephen A. Douglas in the first election. There were only six straight Douglas tickets voted in Elizabeth, three in Rahway and one in Springfield. Although blacks supported the Lincoln ticket in both elections, they were denied access to the mechanisms of formal politics.

In 1861, the Democrats gained control of the legislature and the statehouse with the election of Joel Parker (1816–1888) as governor. In 1863, after reaching its highest degree of support and power in New Jersey, the Democrats passed peace resolutions, opposing the emancipation of the slaves, and asked the federal government to appoint a peace commission to meet southern representatives and end the war. Two years later, they refused to ratify the Thirteenth Amendment, which abolished slavery.

Two of the most outspoken Democratic critics of Lincoln, blacks and the war had connections to Union County: David Naar and Democratic senator James Jenkins of Rahway. Naar was a former Democratic mayor of Elizabethtown and editor/owner of the Trenton *Daily True American*. A Sephardic Jew, he was a spokesman for the prosouthern, antiabolition element of his party. His newspaper, along with the Democratic *Plainfield Gazette* newspaper, published articles sympathetic to the South, which resulted in a statewide boycott mandated by a grand jury sitting at Trenton on September 25, 1861. Both newspapers, along with four others, were censured for alleged treasonable utterances. The grand jury urged the people of New Jersey to boycott all six newspapers. During his one-year tenure (1864–1865) in the state senate, James Jenkins introduced a controversial bounty bill, forbidding payments to all black Civil War volunteers and recruits in New Jersey. The bill failed to pass.

The results of the presidential election of 1864 may have been different had New Jersey troops been permitted to vote in the field. Private Walter Dunn of Plainfield had this to say about the Democratic-controlled legislature that feared strong support for Lincoln among soldiers:

> *As to my coming home to vote, I do not expect to. Men are being sent home from nearly all the northern states for that purpose but if a man belongs to New Jersey he can't go, as the state has made no provisions for her soldiers to vote. Her state Legislature would not pass a Bill, where by her soldiers could be represented at the Ballot Box and of all that has been done for the soldiers, that little contemptible state has done the least.*[5]

While stationed near Berryville, Private Edward C. Jones of Plainfield reported in a September 1864 letter written to his father that a vote taken among the men in his regiment yielded 143 for Lincoln, 75 for McClellan and 30 undecided.

Lincoln lost New Jersey again in 1864 when voters cast its 7 electoral votes for General George B. McClellan, who had earned distinction for his Civil War military service. McClellan carried Elizabeth with 366 votes, while the more Republican-leaning Plainfield supported President Lincoln with a plurality of 159 votes. In the state election, the Democrats carried Union

County, electing James Jenkins of Rahway to the state senate and Philip Dougherty and Joseph T. Crowell (Rahway) to the assembly. In later years, Crowell switched his loyalties to the Republicans.

In 1865, the Democratic legislature refused to ratify the Thirteenth Amendment, abolishing slavery. This motivated blacks throughout the state to redouble their efforts to acquire the ballot. In the summer of 1865, a State Convention of Colored Men met in Trenton and formed an Equal Rights League of New Jersey. A year later, they turned to General Benjamin Butler, popular among New Jersey black veterans, for help in securing voting rights:

> *Gen. Butler arrived at Elizabeth on the 12th inst. It is believed he is on professional business for the colored men of New Jersey, he having been employed by them as counsel, arranging the programme for their application, to be allowed the right of suffrage at the fall elections. By the new Registry Law all voters must be registered, and the inspectors have to take an oath that they will support the Constitution of the State of New Jersey, and by it only whites are allowed to vote. We do not see that there is any great chance for success at present.*[6]

In 1866, the Republican Party—the party of Lincoln—elected Marcus L. Ward and regained control of the legislature. They ratified the Fourteenth Amendment, which guaranteed the citizenship rights of everyone born in the United States. But even this legislature refused to give the franchise to New Jersey blacks. After the Republicans lost control in 1868, the legislature rescinded its ratification of the Fourteenth Amendment. It took the Fifteenth Amendment in 1870 to finally restore suffrage to New Jersey's blacks. In 1875, the word "white" was removed from the voter qualifications in the state constitution.

Chapter 2

Union County Regiments, Recruitment and Enlistments

After the Civil War erupted on April 12, 1861, the government made its initial request to the states for troops; New Jersey was the first to meet its obligation. Union County was not represented by any organized body of troops in the first militia sent out for three months' service in response to the initial request. The county answered later calls for troops with the organization of eleven companies sent for service in seven New Jersey regiments. There is a lack of scholarship focused on black soldiers, many described as mulatto (mixed race), who enlisted in the county's presumed all-white companies. Racial identity was not easily detected: "Quite a number of mulattoes served in white regiments, some as officers; they were so light in complexion that their true race connection could not be told...There were several among the Pennsylvania troops, and not a few in the New York and Massachusetts regiments."[7] Greater accessibility and firsthand examination of service records, letters, Civil War–era African American newspapers and other documents have made the task of determining racial identity of soldiers less daunting.

In May 1861, three New Jersey regiments were formed and designated the First, Second and Third New Jersey Volunteer Regiments. Union County had three companies in these regiments, including Company A, in the First Regiment, Company A in the Second Regiment and Company K in the Third Regiment. Robert J. Carroll of Elizabeth was promoted to corporal in Company K on July 1, 1862, and reduced in rank on December 24, 1862. William Olmstead served in Company A, First Regiment, from May 21,

Above, left: Edward S. Dow enlisted as a corporal in Company I, Fifth New York Cavalry on October 31, 1861, and was later reduced to rank of private. *Courtesy Steve Meadow Collection.*

Above, right: William B. Mason (1845–1916) enlisted as a private in Company I, Ninth Connecticut Infantry in 1861. *Courtesy New Jersey State Archives.*

1861, to December 28, 1863. A combined total of fifty-one blacks enlisted in the three regiments. Ten were killed in action or died of disease.

The Ninth Regiment, dubbed the "Jersey Blues," was organized under an act of Congress on July 22, 1861. The regiment contained Company G and Company K from the county. The operations of the Ninth were confined to the states of North Carolina, South Carolina and Virginia. About 146 Union County black recruits participated in the Ninth's approximately thirty engagements. David Higgins of Rahway served in Company G and was later recruited into Company B, Forty-first Infantry USCT. William J. Ward served in Company G and, after receiving a promotion in another regiment, was reduced in rank on October 21, 1862. Ward was promoted to corporal after reenlisting in Company I, Nineteenth Infantry USCT. About 22 blacks died of wounds received in action and 4 from typhoid fever or diarrhea contracted as a result of poor camp conditions.

New Jersey's Eleventh Regiment was organized on July 7, 1862, in response to President Lincoln's 1862 call for 300,000 additional volunteers to serve for three years. The supply of volunteers had slowed to a trickle,

Robert J. Carroll of Elizabeth served as a hospital steward in the United States Army from 1863 to 1865. *Courtesy Kenneth M. Carroll, M.D. Collection.*

William H. Olmstead served in New Jersey, New York and United States Colored Troops Regiments. *Courtesy Dennis Buttacavoli Collection.*

Corporal David S.C. Higgins served in Company K, Ninth New Jersey Infantry and Company B, Forty-first Infantry USCT. *Courtesy U.S. Army Military History Institute.*

Corporal William J. Ward (1843–1884) of Company I, Nineteenth Infantry USCT was wounded at Walthall, Virginia, on May 6, 1864. *Courtesy New Jersey State Archives.*

John van Horn (1837–1901) of Plainfield enlisted as a private in Company A, Ninth New York Heavy Artillery. *Courtesy John Kuhl Collection.*

and military service had become less attractive. With more aggressive recruiting programs in place, blacks enlisted for service in the two companies organized in Union County, B and D. The reputation of the regiment for fighting qualities was maintained through all their campaigns to the surrender of General Lee and the close of the war. The Eleventh participated in twenty-nine engagements and suffered tremendous losses.

Companies C and E of the Fourteenth Regiment were from Union County. The regiment was mustered into service near Freehold, New Jersey, on August 26, 1862. The regiment linked up with the Army of the Potomac in 1863 and fought with them in all of its battles: the Wilderness, Spotsylvania, Cold Harbor, Petersburg, Monocacy, Sheridan's Shenandoah Valley campaign, back to Petersburg and on to the triumphant end at Appomattox. Known as the "fighting regiment," the Fourteenth ranked in the top ten of Union regiments that suffered significant casualties.

A national draft was adopted on March 3, 1863. Men between the ages of twenty and forty-five were required to serve or provide a substitute. New Jersey sought and was granted permission to enlist its quota of men in lieu of a draft. Through the provision of bounties, Governor Joel Parker prevented the use of conscription to fill military quotas in 1863. However, in 1864, the draft went into effect.

Black enlistments increased substantially after bounties for recruits were offered by Union County, the City of Elizabeth ward authorities, Rahway and Westfield. The Resolution of the Board of Chosen Freeholders was adopted on August 11, 1862, authorizing a committee to make bounty payments to volunteers.[8]

A second resolution was adopted on December 1, 1863, authorizing payment of $300 cash bounties to fifty-two recruits drafted into service on May 20, 1864. A registry dated December 30, 1863, lists the names of fifteen "Colored" volunteers who received bounties ranging from $250 to $300.

State of New Jersey,

EXECUTIVE DEPARTMENT,
November 25, 1863.

DULY AUTHORIZED AGENTS to obtain recruits for old regiments, will receive for each veteran recruit $25, and for a new recruit $15, to be paid by the U. S. Disbursing Officer, at Trenton, upon muster. Where bounties are raised by townships, the Governor of this State will give authority to one person in a township, to act as such agent, upon written request from the township committee. Where bounties are raised by a county, the request must be made by the Board of Chosen Freeholders or their Committee. Where bounties are raised by a city, the request must be made by the Mayor and Common Council. The county or city authorities must designate the number of agents desired, which will not exceed one from each township or ward.

If no action be taken by the above named authorities within a reasonable time, the Governor will appoint without such request. It is hoped that the nominations for agents will be forwarded immediately. The nominations will be subject to the approval of the Governor.

Instructions will be given to the Agents upon their appointment.

JOEL PARKER,
Governor of New Jersey.

nov25-2

Above, left: Governor Joel Parker issued this order to county and city authorities to nominate duly authorized bounty agents. *Courtesy New Jersey State Archives.*

Above, right: William G. Marsh, promoted corporal of Company B, Thirtieth New Jersey Infantry, was reduced to the rank of private. *Courtesy Patrick A. Schroeder Collection.*

Company B of New Jersey's Thirtieth Infantry was organized after President Lincoln's August 4, 1862 order for a draft of 10,478 to serve for nine months. The total strength of Company B was 102. Of that number, 85 have been identified as black. (See Appendix A). Declines in white recruits, along with the implementation of the bounty system, were major factors in the unusually high number of black enlistments.

Joseph T. Crowell (1817–1891), a Democratic senator (later Republican) from Union County, was the authorized bounty agent for the city of Rahway. A Certificate of Military Service was required before issuance of bounty payments to recruits. Crowell wrote a letter to New Jersey adjutant general Robert F. Stockton on June 19, 1865, verifying that the wives of ten "Colored Volunteers" from Rahway had exhibited marriage certificates from the commanding officer of their husbands' respective companies. The wives sought payment on behalf of their husbands who were mustered into service in "Colored" regiments raised at Camp William Penn in Cheltenham, Pennsylvania.

After the second call came for volunteers, the Committee on Enlistment and County Fund for the Township of Westfield was appointed at a public meeting on August 11, 1862. Gideon Ludlow, a former slave owner, served

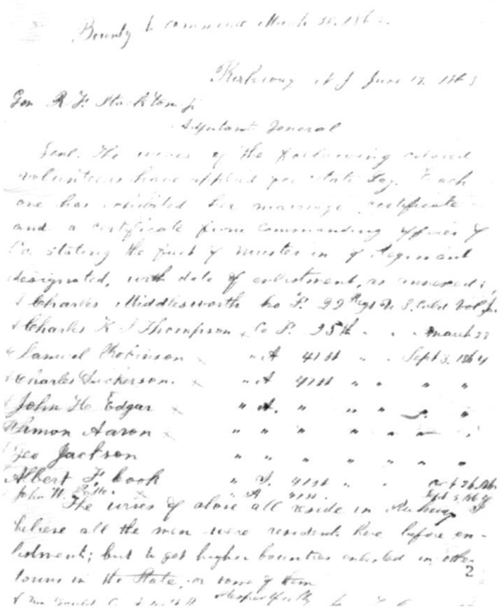

Above, left: Joseph T. Crowell's letter verifying state pay eligibility of Rahway wives of "colored" volunteers. *Courtesy New Jersey State Archives.*

Above, right: John van Pelt, born in Elizabeth, enlisted in Company C, Fourth New York Heavy Artillery. *Courtesy Richard K. Tibbals Collection.*

as chairman of the township's Civil War Board. The Rahway Bank loaned Westfield $10,000 for the purchase of substitutes at amounts ranging from $200 to $400 per man.

Credit for a large number of black men, such as John W. van Pelt of Elizabeth, went to other states, including Connecticut, Delaware, Massachusetts, New York, Pennsylvania and Washington, D.C.

Chapter 3

United States Colored Troops (USCT) 1862–66

The initial Federal program to admit blacks into the Union army met with fierce opposition. However, this changed shortly afterward due to a series of events. Declining enlistments, heavy battle losses, desertions, discharges, the authorization of a draft, as well as the realization that the war would take more time and resources than expected were just some of the issues confronting President Lincoln and the Union army. Black leaders and abolitionists brought pressure upon Congress to lift the army's prohibition of "Negroes or Mulattoes," which had been in existence since 1820. On July 17, 1862, Congress passed two acts, allowing the enlistment of blacks. Official enrollment occurred after the September 1862 issuance of the Emancipation Proclamation, which took effect on January 1, 1863.

The Bureau of Colored Troops was established by General Order 143 on May 22, 1863, to facilitate the recruitment of black soldiers to fight for the Union army. Infantry, cavalry, light artillery and heavy artillery units were recruited from states within the Union. The recruits belonged to one central body, the United States Colored Troops (USCT), except for the Twenty-ninth Connecticut Infantry, the Fifty-fourth and Fifty-fifth Massachusetts Infantry Regiments and the Fifth Massachusetts Colored Cavalry Regiment. The four regiments maintained state designations throughout the war.

With the full support of his fellow Democrats who were in control of the state legislature, New Jersey governor Joel Parker refused to organize black troops within the state. A directive was issued by the Federal War Department in Washington on September 19, 1863, with instructions for the mustering of all black recruits into regiments of the USCT. As a way of verifying enlistment, certificates were issued by the state's chief mustering officer. Despite the initial opposition, New Jersey did not hesitate to accept credit for black enlistees after the directive was later modified, giving the superintendent of New Jersey's Recruiting Service authority to enroll and muster black recruits. They were enrolled and mustered in by provost marshals of districts, forwarded to a draft rendezvous in Trenton, transferred to specified depots, assigned to USCT regiments and rated as part of the regular force of the United States Army. Black recruits were represented most heavily in the 22nd Infantry, considered the most "Jersey" of the regiments; the 25th Infantry, the only all-black corps in United States history; the 41st Infantry; and the 127th Infantry. Officers received appointments, commissions and command assignments from the War Department.

Left: William H. Dunn served in Company H, 127th United States Colored Infantry. *Courtesy MOLLUS-MA & U.S. Army Military History Institute.*

Below: Private Robert Bray's Certificate of Service in the United States Colored Troops, Camp William Penn, Chelten Hills, Pennsylvania. *Courtesy New Jersey State Archives.*

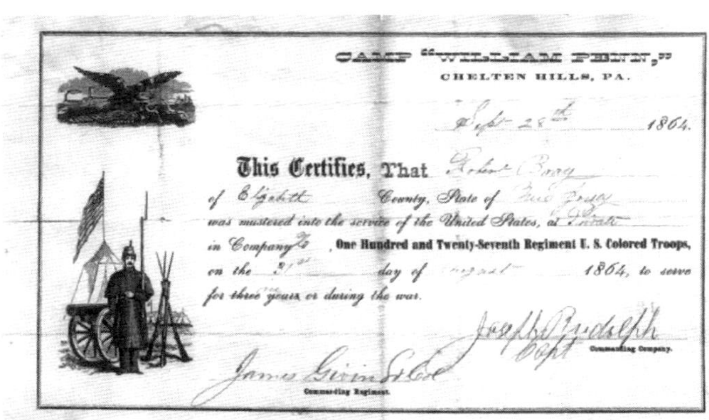

CAMP "WILLIAM PENN,"
CHELTEN HILLS, PA.

Sept 28th 1864.

This Certifies, That Robert Bray of Elizabeth County, State of New Jersey was mustered into the service of the United States, as Private in Company H, One Hundred and Twenty-Seventh Regiment U. S. Colored Troops, on the 31st day of August 1864, to serve for three years or during the war.

[illegible signature] Capt
Commanding Company.

[illegible signature]
Commanding Regiment.

Left: Joseph C. Robinson (1840–1878) was promoted to first lieutenant and adjutant of Company C, New York 106th Infantry on February 4, 1864. *Courtesy Douglas Moore Collection.*

Below: Captain Henry C. Brandt *(far right front)*, described as a mulatto, is pictured with a group of officers in 1865. *Courtesy of U.S. Army Military History Institute.*

From the beginning, blacks were thought to be lesser soldiers and confronted with government-sanctioned discriminatory practices, including subordination in military units, poorer equipment, a lack of assignments to frontline positions and unequal pay scales. Congress passed the Enlistment Act of July 1862, which mandated that white soldiers holding the rank of private should be paid $13.00 a month and $3.50 for clothing. Blacks were accorded $7.00 a month and a $3.00 allocation for clothing. Overwhelming protest from black leaders, and others, forced the passage of the equal-pay bill. Congress reversed itself in June 1864 and authorized "all persons of color who were free" be paid the same wage as white soldiers. The inequity in pay was reversed on March 3, 1865, with

Presentation of Colors to the Twentieth United States Colored Infantry at the Union League House, New York, on March 26, 1864. *Courtesy New York Public Library.*

the passage of the Enrollment Act, authorizing the army to pay all black soldiers the same wage as whites, retroactive to January 1, 1864.

The county's close proximity to the state of New York was a major factor in the number of blacks enlisting in that state's many regiments, including three United States Colored Troops infantry units: the Twentieth, Twenty-sixth and Thirty-first Regiments. New Jersey lost credit for many of these recruits. The Twentieth Infantry, which had the highest number of enlistees, was organized at Riker's Island, New York, on February 18, 1864. On March 5, 1864, 100,000 New Yorkers turned out in Union Square to watch the Union League present colors to a regiment that had been created by New York abolitionists. The presentation of colors was a moving ritual marking the entry of a regiment in service.

The Twenty-sixth Infantry was organized at Riker's Island, New York Harbor, on February 27, 1864, to serve three years. The organization of the Thirty-first Infantry was commenced under Henry C. Ward at Hart's Island, New York Harbor, on April 29, 1864, and completed in Virginia on November 14, 1864. It was mustered into service for three years. The Thirtieth Connecticut Colored Volunteers, while in the process of organization, were merged into this regiment on May 18, 1864.

William E. Potter (1840–1896), a mulatto, was a substitute and captain in Company G, Twelfth New Jersey Infantry and later reduced to rank of private. *Courtesy New Jersey State Archives.*

In June 1863, the War Department announced that it would not commission blacks as line or field officers of "Colored" regiments. In 1863, the Philadelphia Supervisory Committee for Enlistment of Colored Troops responded with the establishment of the Free Military School for Applicants for Commands of Colored Troops to prepare white officers for command of black troops. The core premise of the school was that black soldiers needed white officers. The policy was later reversed with the enrollment of black soldiers who were mostly described as mulattos. During its nine months of operation, December 1863 to September 1864, the school produced 484 officers who served with the USCT. A total of 12 black New Jersey recruits were admitted to the school, 2 withdrew, 2 dropped out and 3 were passed by the Board of Examiners at Washington, D.C.

The names and command recommendations of Union County men appear on the school's Roll of Honor, including Private Henry W. Hand, who entered on January 18, 1864, and upon completion of training, was recommended to rank of captain; Charles H. McKinney, who entered on February 15, 1864; Corporal William H. Cox, who enrolled on February 17, 1864; Henry A. Whitney, who entered as a civilian on January 14, 1864 and was recommended for commission as second lieutenant; and Henry H. Wilson, who enrolled on March 26, 1864. Commissions and promotions were also earned by blacks who did not attend the military school, including John Burns, who was commissioned and promoted as captain in the Forty-eighth Infantry on December 6, 1863.

Lieutenant John H. Simmons of Elizabeth was wounded on July 30, 1864 at Petersburg, Virginia, and died on August 10, 1864. *Courtesy MOLLUS-MA & U.S. Army Military History Institute.*

In 1862, General Benjamin F. Butler's First, Second and Third Louisiana Native Guards were organized from existing free

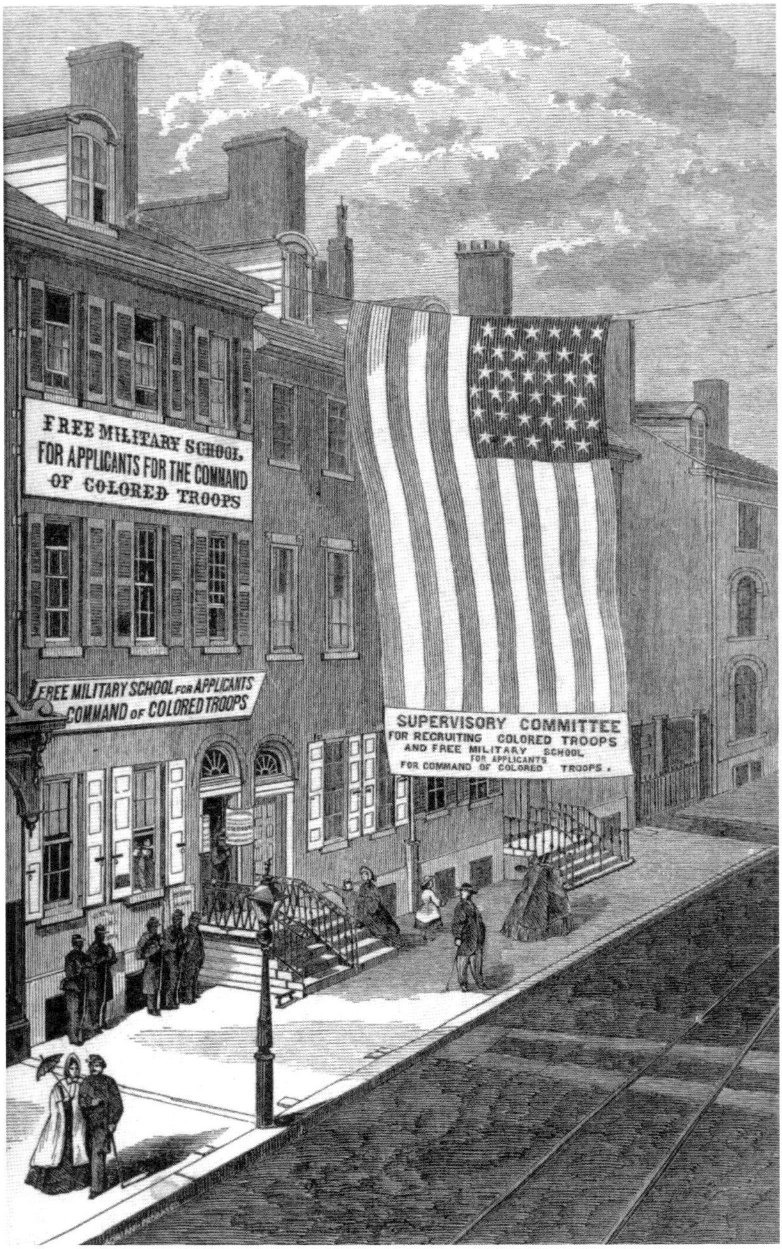

Front of free military school for applicants for commands of colored troops, Philadelphia, 1864. *Courtesy New York Public Library.*

Above, left: Henry S. Vanderveer (1843–1932) enlisted as a musician of Company C, 127th United States Colored Infantry on August 24, 1864. *Courtesy of the Author.*

Above, right: Charles H. Randolph (1844–1918) was commissioned as captain of Company C, 118th United States Colored Infantry on April 11, 1865. *Courtesy U.S. Army Military History Institute.*

Below: Captain John Burns is pictured *(top left)* with other officers of the Forty-eighth Regiment, United States Colored Troops. *Courtesy Roger G. Hunt Collection.*

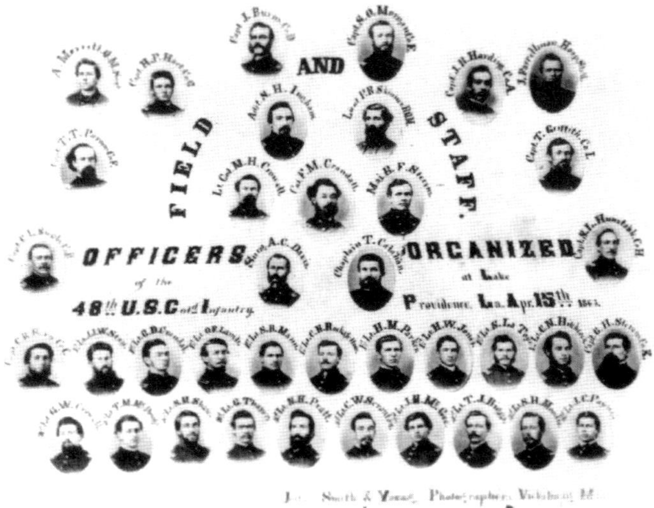

Captain Henry H. Wilson of Company F, Sixteenth Pennsylvania Cavalry, was killed in action at Locust Grove, Virginia, on November 27, 1863. *Courtesy Jim Jezorski Collection.*

Randolph Marsh was promoted to second lieutenant of Company C, Second New Jersey Infantry and later reduced to rank of private. *Courtesy New Jersey State Archives.*

William G. Powers was commissioned first lieutenant of Company G, Twenty-fifth Regiment, United States Colored Troops on March 3, 1864. *Courtesy Bill Gladstone Collection.*

Second Lieutenant Elihu H. Ropes, described as "light" in complexion, resigned after a reduction in rank on November 30, 1865. *Courtesy U.S. Army Military History Institute.*

Henry A. Whitney trained at the free military school for applicants for commands of colored troops, Philadelphia. *Courtesy MOLLUS-MA & U.S. Army Military History Institute.*

black militia units. The following was written into Order Number 40 during the organization of the Corps d' Afrique:

> *The commanding General desires to detail for temporary or permanent duty, the best officers of the army, for the organization, instruction, and discipline of this Corps. With them he is confident that the Corps will render important service to the government. It is not established upon any dogma of equality or other theory, but as a practical and sensible matter of business. The government makes use of mules, horses, uneducated white men in the defence of its institutions; why should not the Negro contribute whatever is in his power, for the cause in which he is as deeply interested as other men? We may properly demand from him whatever service he can render.*[9]

More than seventy-five blacks were commissioned in the three regiments, including Union County's First Lieutenants Theodore Clark, Joseph Jones and George Watson and Captains James H. Ingraham, John C. Holland and David B. Jenkins. Several of those receiving commissions resigned because of tension in the ranks, namely the army's official policy of excluding blacks from leadership positions and officer promotions. General Nathaniel Banks, who was hostile to black officers, replaced them with white officers. William W. Conover of Elizabeth declined his commission and resigned on April 7, 1865.

To date, at least 120 men of African descent have been identified as commissioned officers in the Union army. On April 29, 1866, Hospital Steward George M. Arnold delivered a farewell address to his comrades of the Fourth Infantry United States Colored Troops, urging them to remember the deeds of officers:

> *Let us not forget the officers of our command, who have led us through the struggle. To remember them with affection is part of our duty. We must not forget how they came forward and entered this branch of the service, which, at the commencement, was considered by many a disgraceful thing. Besides this, they know an officer in the colored service was promised no mercy if captured. Having carried us through the storm of battle, not withstanding a liberal share of prejudice from their brother officers associated with white troops, none more than those who slurred them then, envy their laurels and honor now. The bright and glorious record of the officers of the colored service is indelible in the history of the War of the Union. Their names will live and flourish.*[10]

Clockwise from top left: Theodore C. Clark was promoted to first lieutenant of the Fourth United States Colored Cavalry (First Corps d'Afrique) on August 16, 1865. *Courtesy Bill Gladstone Collection*; Henry S. Manning (1834–1910), of Rahway, enlisted as second lieutenant of Company B, Eighty-second, USCT. *Courtesy U.S. Military History Institute;* Bust portrait of Captain William W. Conover, Company G, Fourteenth New Jersey Infantry, with a Sixth Corps badge pinned to his uniform. *Courtesy New Jersey State Archives*; James E. Parker was promoted to first lieutenant of Company K, Twelfth Heavy Artillery, USCT, on August 2, 1864. *Courtesy U.S. Army Military History Institute.*

Black troops participated in every major Union campaign between the periods of 1863 and 1865, except for Sherman's invasion of Georgia. Union County soldiers were well represented at the Battle of the Crater at Petersburg, Virginia, where regiments of the USCT suffered heavy casualties while attempting to break through Confederate lines. Considered one of the most disastrous battles that the Ninth Corps participated in, the Battle at the Crater included nine United States Colored Infantry units, three of which were the Sixth, Nineteenth and the Thirty-ninth. Union County's Privates William Carroll, Nathaniel Day, William Hughes and Peter Marsh were drafted into the Sixth Infantry; Privates George Goodwin, John Harvey, Adolphus Johnson and John H. Johnson were mustered in as substitutes; and Corporals Francis Davis and John Ross, along with Privates William Henry and Samuel Howard, enlisted in July or August 1863. Although eventually defeated, the courageous soldiers were lauded for their bravery by those witnessing the event.

Top: William H.H. Avery was commissioned captain of Company D, Forty-second Infantry, USCT. He resigned on July 28, 1865. *Courtesy Thomas L. Avery.*

Middle: David B. Jenkins was commissioned on September 10, 1863, as a captain in the Corps d'Afrique, dissolved in April 1864. *Courtesy New Jersey State Archives.*

Bottom: John Ryan, a resident of Linden, enlisted as second lieutenant of Company E, 118th Infantry, USCT. *Courtesy New Jersey State Archives.*

A total of 1,327 black soldiers were killed at Petersburg, including Thomas Clark of Westfield on June 18, 1865; Samuel S. Cromwell of Rahway on June 28, 1864; Private Charles Dickinson of Rahway, June 6, 1864; Jacob D. van Pelt of Elizabeth on July 9, 1863; John Warfield of Rahway on January 8, 1864; and Second Lieutenant John Ryan of the 118th Infantry. Among the wounded were Corporal John Ross on June 15, 1864, First Lieutenant David W. Carr on June 18, 1864; Anthony Randolph of Rahway on August 18, 1864; Rufus L. Robinson of Westfield on April 2, 1865; and Corporal John V.M. Sutphin of Westfield on August 18, 1864.

The Battle of New Market Heights, Virginia (Chaffin's Farm), was one of the most heroic engagements involving blacks. The battle took place outside of Richmond, Virginia, on September 29–30, 1864. It was part of the Richmond-Petersburg Campaign, which lasted from June 1864 to March 1865. The regiment entered the battle with 367, rank and file. Of this number, 3 officers and 39 men were killed, 11 officers and 150 were wounded and 7 went missing. There was an aggregate of 210, which was more than 62 percent of its strength. Second Lieutenant James W. Fisher of Elizabeth was wounded at Chaffin's Farm, Virginia, on September 29, 1864, and discharged as a result of those wounds on April 30, 1865. Private Samuel Sharp of Linden was wounded in the forearm at Chaffin's Farm on September 29, 1864.

The Twenty-second Infantry, the only all-black USCT regiment, Duncan's Brigade, before Petersburg. *Courtesy of the author.*

Black soldiers bury their dead after one of the terrible battles before Petersburg. *Courtesy of the author.*

The army Medal of Honor (MOH) was created by the United States Congress in 1861. In 1973, after years of being hidden away in unattended archives, the United States Senate ordered the citations compiled and printed, in book form, as the *Committee on Veteran's Affairs, U. S. Senate, Medal of Honor Recipients: 1863–1973.* Several Union County soldiers were recipients of the MOH for bravery and heroism during the Civil War:

John Corcoran
Private
Third Battle of Petersburg, VA, April 2, 1865
One of a detachment of 20 picked artillery men who voluntarily accompanied an infantry assaulting party, and who turned upon the enemy the guns captured in the assault.

Francis B. Hall
Chaplain
Salem Heights, VA, May 3, 1863
Voluntarily exposed himself to a heavy fire during the thickest of the fight and carried wounded men to the rear for treatment and attendance.

John Johnson
Private
Battle of Antietam, MD, and Battle of Fredericksburg, VA, September 17, 1862 and December 13, 1862
Conspicuous gallantry in battle in which he was severely wounded. While serving as cannoneer he manned the positions of fallen gunners.

John Kane
Corporal
Third Battle of Petersburg, VA, April 2, 1865
Gallantry as color bearer in the assault on Fort Gregg.

Charles Oliver
Sergeant
Battle of Fort Stedman, Petersburg, VA, March 25, 1864
Capture of flag of 31st Georgia Infantry (CSA).

John H. Robinson
Private
Battle of Gettysburg, PA, July 3, 1863
Capture of flag of 57th Virginia Infantry (CSA)

William H. Williams
Private
Battle of Peachtree Creek, GA, July 20, 1864
For voluntarily going beyond the lines to observe the enemy and aiding a wounded comrade.

The Butler Medal, also known as the Army of the James Medal, was created by Benjamin F. Butler for black troops after their show of bravery and courage during the Battle of New Market Heights. There were approximately two hundred Butler medals made and given to soldiers. Although there is no list of the names of Union County soldiers who were recipients of the Butler medal, those commissioned as officers of the Butler Louisiana/Louisiana Native Guard Regiments include Captain James H. Ingraham, First Regiment; Lieutenants George T. Watson and Joseph Jones, Second Regiment; and Captain John J. Holland, Third Regiment.

Army Medal of Honor *(left)* and the Butler Medal of Honor *(right)*, named for General Benjamin F. Butler, the only medal ever struck to honor black troops. *Courtesy of the author.*

Three months after awarding the medals, Butler was relieved of his command of the Army of the James, and the soldiers were told they could not display the medal on their uniforms. The Butler Medal was not recognized by the government, which makes knowledge of the medal and who received it nearly impossible to determine. All future attempts to gain recognition for the recipients were thwarted by the Department of Defense, who issued this statement in 1981: "The Department takes the position that large numbers of unofficial medals were privately issued to members of the Armed Forces of the United States between 1861 and 1865. The Butler Medal was but one of the many in this category."[11]

Fighting in 449 engagements, of which 39 were major battles, black soldiers proved themselves as reputable soldiers. They were finally honored with the erection of an African American Civil War Memorial bearing their names. The unveiling was held in Washington, D.C., on July 15–19, 1998.

Chapter 4

Sailors: United States Navy and Marine Corps

The United States Navy Act of 1813 provided for the enlistment of free "persons of color" in the service. A melting pot that brought together all different nationalities, races and age groups, it is estimated that about 8 percent of the 118,000 men who entered the U.S. Navy during the Civil War were of African ancestry.

Despite the essential role they played in and off the battlefield, extensive research and documentation of the experiences of blacks in the United States Navy during the Civil War did not receive serious attention until 1993, when a team from Howard University, the U.S. Department of the Navy and the U.S. National Park Service formed a partnership to research and document the service and experiences of blacks in the Civil War. The result of this team effort, the Howard University Sailors Project, was the creation of the Civil War Soldiers and Sailors (CWSS) database of about 18,000 African American sailors. The CWSS database contains the names and records of 433 sailors of African ancestry credited to New Jersey. Of that number, 22 were identified as Union County residents. Additional names and service records were obtained from documents housed at the Union County Office of Veterans Affairs and other local sources.

Prior to February 24, 1864, credit for enlistment and service in the naval forces was not given to states. Instead, under the provisions of Section Nine of an Act of Congress, approved July 4, 1864, all enlistments into the naval service or into the Marine Corps of the United States were to be credited to the town, township, county, ward or election district in which the enlisted

Above, left: Private William A. Scott, an ordinary seaman, U.S. Navy, also served in Company E, Seventh Regiment, New York State Militia. *Courtesy U.S. Army Military History Institute.*

Above, right: George W. Randolph, a Plainfield native, enlisted as a landsman in the U.S. Navy on May 31, 1864. *Courtesy of the author.*

men were or may have been enrolled and liable to duty. Those credited would be determined by a commission of two, of whom the state named one and the secretary of war the other. William Scott of Elizabeth and George W. Randolph of Plainfield enlisted in the navy after the act went into effect. Both were credited to New Jersey.

While determining the African ancestry of both soldiers and sailors was challenging, identification of sailors was less difficult. The navy provided a description of enlistees, including color of hair, eyes, skin and complexion (Negro, colored, black, mulatto), at the time of enlistment. In some instances, very light-skinned blacks were described as "dark," even when they were clearly not, as demonstrated by the photos of Henry C. Tilton and George W. Ackerman of Elizabeth. Both were described as dark on their service records.

In addition to the enlistees of African ancestry born in Union County, many others were born in Europe, the West Indies and Canada, settling in the county after mustering out of the navy. William H. Simms, a resident of

Above, left: Henry C. Tilton, landsman, U.S. Navy, served aboard the USS *Genesee* from September 6, 1864, to April 26, 1865. *Courtesy New Jersey State Archives.*

Above, right: George W. Ackerman, a seaman, U.S. Navy, also was a private in Battery F, First Regiment, Pennsylvania Light Artillery. *Courtesy Leister Collection.*

Plainfield, was born in Canada; Rahway resident Sylvester Doremus was born in England; Joseph King was born in Lisbon, Portugal, and settled in Rahway; George A. Sutphen was born in Martinique and settled in Plainfield; William J. Gould of Rahway was born in Jamaica; and Edward Du Bois, born in Nassau, New Providence, lived in Elizabeth. In the event of their capture or imprisonment in a Rebel camp, sailors at sea were issued a Certificate of Citizenship for verification and protection.

Although the navy did not create a separate administrative body equivalent to the army's Bureau for Colored Troops, sailors, like their army counterparts, were confronted with discriminatory policies and practices. The guidelines for recruiting and rating black sailors reinforced the prejudices of recruiters, naval officers and white enlisted men. The seafaring experience and skills of black seamen was regularly ignored. Ranks and positions held by black sailors, beginning with the lowest, was boy third class, boy second class and boy first class; landsman; ordinary seaman; seaman; petty officers, mostly stewards and cooks; firemen; or surgeon assistants.[12] Contraband sailors

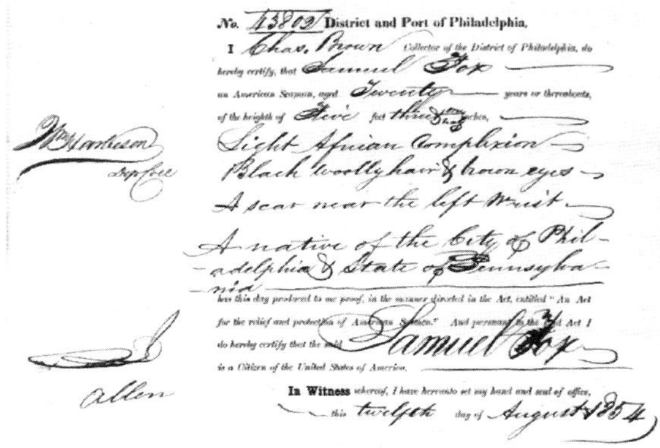

No. 13802 District and Port of Philadelphia.
I Chas. Brown Collector of the District of Philadelphia, do hereby certify, that Samuel Fox an American Seaman, aged Twenty years or thereabouts, of the height of Five feet three inches, Light African Complexion Black woolly hair & brown eyes A scar near the left wrist A native of the City of Philadelphia & State of Pennsylvania has this day produced to me proof, in the manner directed in the Act, entitled "An Act for the relief and protection of American Seamen." And pursuant to the said Act I do hereby certify that the said Samuel Fox is a Citizen of the United States of America.
In Witness whereof, I have hereunto set my hand and seal of office, this twelfth day of August 1854

Above, left: William H. Simms was a seaman aboard the USS *North Carolina* and a landsman on the USS *Pontoosuc*. *Courtesy Thomas P. Lowry Collection.*

Above, right: A Seaman's Protection Certificate was issued to black sailors as verification of United States citizenship in the event of capture or impressments. *Courtesy of the author.*

represented a large segment of the navy's entire enlisted force, occupying the lowest ranks of boys and landsmen. Michael Breen, William Zabriskie and William H. Decamp were among those receiving the lowest rank of boy at the time of their enlistment. The majority of Union County enlistees were ranked landsman or seaman.

There were no black commissioned U.S. naval officers during the Civil War. Some held one of four prestigious petty officer ratings: boatswain's mate, captain of the hold, master at arms and quartermaster. Vessels, where de facto segregation prevailed, offered opportunities for advancement. Henry W. Hand attended the Free Military School for Applicants for the Command of Colored Troops and was promoted as acting master in the U.S. volunteer navy on board the USS *New Hampshire*.

Blacks served on nearly all seven hundred navy vessels, including the USS *Monitor*. On March 8–9, 1862, a few Union County sailors participated in the war's first major naval battle in which the Confederate ironclad *Merrimack* battled with the Union ironclad *Monitor* in the harbor at Hampton Roads, Virginia. The *Monitor* carried the day, but the top-heavy ship later sank in a storm. Its remains were discovered in 1973. In 2003, its revolving gun turret was raised from the sea floor.

Lieutenants Theodore C. Clark (Rahway) and Charles Benson (Plainfield) were among the officers of African descent that served in the First Battalion

William H. De Camp was a fireman first class, U.S. Navy, aboard the USS *Rhode Island* from July 16, 1861, to January 18, 1862. *Courtesy Gil Barrett Collection.*

Acting Master Henry W. Hand aboard the USS *New Hampshire. Courtesy MOLLUS-MA & U.S. Army Military History Institute.*

of Cavalry, Mississippi Marine Brigade (MMB), a unit raised directly by the Federal government. Like the U.S. Navy, it was a part of the military with warships during the Civil War. These warships operated river patrol gunboats and a vessel known as a "ram," which carried troops and horses during the war. The patrol, limited almost entirely to the Mississippi River, was operated by sailors. The soldiers on board served in a capacity similar to that of the U.S. marines aboard navy vessels. In August 1864, the War Department discharged the officers, scattered the vessels among various ports and removed the MMB troops from the ships, turning them into a standard fighting regiment based in Vicksburg, Virginia. The name of the unit was changed to the First Mississippi Marine Brigade.

The navy and marine corps' Medal of Honor was created for enlisted men by Secretary of the Navy Gideon Wells on December 16, 1861. Sailors served with heroism and were essential to many Union victories. Union County sailors listed below earned the United States Navy Medal of Honor for various acts of courage during the Civil War. Their names are followed by their rank and rate, if known, the vessel or unit on which they served, state accredited, and the citation:

Henry W. Hand *(lower deck, far right)* served in a United States Colored Troops regiment. *Courtesy MOLLUS-MA & U.S. Military History Institute.*

Above: Officers and crew of the *Monitor* battled the Confederate's *Merrimac* to a standoff in July 1862. *Courtesy the Library of Congress.*

Below: A group of officers on deck of the USS *Monitor*. *Courtesy Richard Coles, Union County Historical Society.*

Lieutenant Theodore C. Clark *(second, first row)* with other officers of African descent, Mississippi Marine Brigade. *Courtesy MOLLUS-MA & U.S. Military History Institute.*

James H. Avery
Seaman, USS *Metacomet*, New York
Citation: One of boat crew which went to rescue USS *Monitor Tecumseh* when that vessel was struck by a torpedo in passing the enemy forts in Mobile Bay, Alabama, August 5, 1864.

Charles H. Baldwin
Coal heaver, USS *Wyalusing*
Citation: Volunteered for hazardous mission at Roanoke River, North Carolina, August 5, 1864.

John Michael Burns
Seaman, USS *Lackawanna*
Citation: On board during successful attacks against Fort Morgan, rebel gunboats and the ram Tennessee in Mobile Bay, August 5, 1864.

William H. Dunn
Quartermaster, USS *Monadnock*
Citation: On board during several attacks in Fort Fisher, December 24–25, 1864 and January 13–15, 1865.

Robert Graham
Landsman, USS *Tacony*
Citation: During the capture of Plymouth, North Carolina, distinguished himself by a display of coolness when he participated in landing and spiking a 9–inch gun while under a devastating fire from enemy musketry, October 31, 1864.

Charles Hawkins
Seaman, USS *Agawam*
Citation: One of the volunteer crew of a powder boat which was exploded near Fort Fisher, December 23, 1864.

William H. Jones
Landsman, USS *Richmond*
Citation: As captain of a gun on board the ship during action against rebel forts and gunboats and with the ram Tennessee in Mobile Bay, Alabama, August 5, 1864.

John McDonald
Boatswain's mate, USS *Baron De Kalb*, Massachusetts
Citation: Distinguished himself in various actions while serving on board during the Yazoo River Expedition, December 23–27 and December 1862.

John McFarland
Landsman, USS *Hartford*, Massachusetts
Citation: For remaining steadfast while stationed at the wheel of the vessel during successful action against Fort Morgan, rebel gunboats and the ram in Tennessee in Mobile Bay, Alabama, August 5, 1864.

George W. Moore
Seaman, USS *Rhode Island*, Pennsylvania
Citation: Participated in the hazardous task of rescuing the officers and crew of the sinking Monitor at Cape Hatteras, December 30, 1862.

Thomas Smith
Seaman, USS *Magnolia*
Citation: For remarkable efforts in assisting transport of the gun at St. Marks, Florida, March 3, 1865.

John Williams
Second boatswain mate, USS *Mohican*, New Jersey
Citation: As captain of an 11 inch gun aboard ship, cool and courageous actions at his battle station, maintained a steady fire against the heavily defended Forts Beauregard and Walker on Hilton Head, and against ships of the Confederate Fleet at Hilton Head, South Carolina, November 7, 1861.

Nearly 150 years after the end of the Civil War, the story of the black naval experience is still unfolding. This is a partial narrative of the lives and naval experiences of Union County blacks. Besides the Civil War Soldiers and Sailors (CWSS) database, examination of military records housed at the Military History Institute at Saratoga Springs, New York, and the Union County Office of Veteran Affairs were valuable resources in piecing together this story.

Chapter 5

Rahway Contributions to the War Effort

The patriotic citizens of the City of Rahway demonstrated an exceptional commitment to President Abraham Lincoln and the Union cause, as demonstrated by words and deeds throughout the period of the Civil War. Despite Rahway's profitable and dependent economic ties to southern markets, the city council of Rahway and its citizens were early supporters of the Union cause, as demonstrated by the passage of a resolution on May 7, 1861, in response to Lincoln's call for seventy-five-thousand troops from each state to help subdue the rebellion of the South:

> *Where as The President of the United States has issued his Proclamation announcing that a portion of the Southern States are in open rebellion against the General Government, and are seeking its overthrow and destruction, setting at naught its authority, seizing Government, as well as private property, placing the lives of loyal citizens at jeopardy, and insulting and degrading the Flag of the Country.*
>
> *Be it resolved by the Common Council of Rahway that we tender to the President of the United States our entire devotion to the Constitution and Laws, and will with our laws, Fortune, and honor defend the Government in its determination to crush rebellion, defend the honor and integrity of the Union, and protect the Stars and Stripes from the insults of Rebel and traitors at home, or a honorable enemy abroad.*
>
> *That however much we may deplore the ravages of Civil War, we believe it to be the duty of the Government to prosecute the present war to the fullest*

extent of its means in men & money until rebellion is subdued and peace and harmony are returned throughout the land.[13]

Rahway distinguished itself as the only other Union County town—Elizabeth being the other—to recruit and organize a battery from its local diversified citizenry. Colonel John J. Cladek, a Rahway resident, was responsible for recruiting the local boys, which included a good representation of blacks. According to minutes taken at a meeting of the Board of the Union Brigade, in Union County, New Jersey, held on Wednesday afternoon, March 27, 1861, at the "Town Halle" City of Rahway:

An application was received from the uniformed companies of the City of Rahway praying to be set off into an Independent Battalion to be called the City Battalion of Rahway signed by sixty men of the two companies now existing, and 38 more men not belonging to any company pledged to join our independent Battalion.[14]

New Jersey state officials replied that they could not accept the Rahway offer because they were taking no artillery or cavalry units. Soon after this rejection notice was received from the state, an offer arrived from New York, asking the group to join ranks with the Ninth Regiment of New York. The offer was accepted and Rahway's Company K of the Ninth New York State Militia, later Eighty-third New York Volunteers, was organized. Although equipment had arrived in June, the U.S. government had not been able to immediately supply the new soldiers with standard blue army-issue clothing. State Democratic senator Joseph T. Crowell, a Rahway printer and editor, came forward and donated $3,000 to outfit the soldiers in uniforms modeled after those worn by the north African army of Emperor Napoleon III of France, known as Zouave uniforms. The word *Zouave* (pronounced *Zu* as in look; *ov* as in suave, with the stress on the *ov*) is from an Algerian tribe named Berber Zwawa. While the Algerian soldiers in the French infantry units were known for their flashy uniforms and quick-spirited drill, the uniforms were more likely selected because of the infantry's reputation for military excellence and bravery. Rahway soldiers accepted the belief that the uniforms boosted morale and confidence, helping the units become known as fierce and dependable fighters.[15]

On Sunday, June 9, 1861, the company, comprised of thirty-nine recruits, formed at the armory and marched off to hear a rallying sermon delivered by the Reverend William Rollinson, pastor of the First Baptist Church of

Left: Corporal George H. Brown of the New York Sixth Light Artillery wearing a cropped Zouvac-style jacket. *Courtesy U.S. Army Military History Institute.*

Below: Uniform of Colonel Geary's artillery (General Banks Division). *Courtesy of the author.*

Four soldiers wearing variations of Zouvac uniforms. *Courtesy Richard T. Coles, Union County Historical Society.*

Rahway. The sermon helped solidify a sense of duty to Rahway and the nation. The men left the church and headed for the nearby home of John R. Chapin, the group's commander and organizer, who turned the company over to the command of First Lieutenant Walter M. Bramhall.

Among the other local officers chosen were Joseph W. Martin, second lieutenant; Guyon Merrick, second sergeant; James Monarch, fourth sergeant; John W. Brown, first corporal; and George Brown Jr., second corporal. Company K left Rahway four days later, June 13, 1861.

The company reached Washington, D.C., on November 30, 1861. They were given orders to join General Joseph E. "Fighting Joe" Hooker's Division at Budd's Ferry. On December 22, 1861, the company was detached from the Ninth Regiment and became the Sixth New York Light Artillery Battery, commonly known as Bramhall's Battery of Light Artillery. Lieutenant Walter M. Bramhall commanded the Peninsular Campaign, where the battery achieved honorable distinction. Captain Bramhall resigned on February 16, 1863. He was succeeded by Lieutenant Joseph W. Martin, who was

Left: Captain Joseph W. Martin commanded the New York Sixth Light Artillery at Gettysburg from June 8, 1863, to February 15, 1865. *Courtesy U.S. Army Military History Institute.*

Below: Moses P. Clark *(standing sixth from left)* with other officers of the New York Sixth Light Artillery. *Courtesy MOLLUS-MA & U.S. Army Military History Institute.*

Corporal Thompson Thorn served with the horse artillery in the Army of the Potomac Cavalry Corps. *Courtesy Clark B. Hall Collection.*

honorably discharged at the expiration of his term of service on February 16, 1865. Lieutenant Martin was replaced with another Rahway resident, Lieutenant Moses P. Clark, under whose command the battery returned at the end of the war.

In March 1863, General William F. Barry honored Bramhall's Battery by making it a flying battery. The high-profile outfit served as horse artillery in the Army of the Potomac Cavalry Corps. At Gettysburg, the battery was attached to the First Brigade Horse Artillery, Kilpatrick's Division.

The battery, fighting exclusively with the Army of the Potomac, was attached to the cavalry corps as a six-gun horse artillery for most of the war. It was the only outfit to be so designated. From then on, the unit became known as the Sixth New York Horse Battery. Their battle honors include Williamsburg, Chancellorsville, Beverly Ford, Gettysburg, Brandy Station, Wilderness, Sheridan's Raid, Cedar Creek and the Shenandoah Valley campaign. The sixth earned a reputation as a reliable and efficient battery.

After the war, the State of New Jersey tried to have the command, with all its victories, credited to the state. New York and members of the company balked at the idea. The battery has remained in the history books as the Sixth

New York Horse Battery. In tribute to the battery, the New York Monuments Commission erected its own monument at the Gettysburg Battlefield.

The patriotism of Rahway's black soldiers and citizens did not end with their enlistments in the Sixth Independent Battery. When President Lincoln called for 300,000 volunteers in 1862, within one year, 104 additional young Rahway men enlisted in the Union army. By 1865, nearly one-tenth of the Rahway population had participated in the Civil War.

A significant number of gravestones inscribed with the letters USCT (United States Colored Troops) can be found in the town's historic cemeteries, Rahway Cemetery and Hazelwood Cemetery. The inscriptions are evidence of the many unknown and forgotten black soldiers who fought courageously on behalf of the Union.

On April 17, 1865, two days after receiving news of President Abraham Lincoln assassination on April 15, 1865, a shocked and grieving board of councilmen of the city of Rahway met and passed a resolution paying tribute to a president held in high esteem:

> *Whereas the melancholy intelligence has reached us that the Nation's Chief Magistrate has been stricken down by the hand of violence, therefore,*
>
> *Resolved, That in the death of our late President we recognize the loss of one who was preeminently the honest man, the patriot and the martyr, and that we unite our grief with the grief of our citizens in this dark hour of national bereavement.*
>
> *Resolved, That our citizens are requested in accordance with the recommendation of the acting Secretary of State, to meet in their respective*

Anthony Hall's grave marker at Rahway Cemetery. *Courtesy of the author.*

The Rahway Civil War Monument, dedicated on October 12, 1913, commemorates the valor of its soldiers and sailors. *Courtesy Richard T. Koles.*

> *places of worship on Wednesday the 19th...at 12 o'clock to solemnize the occasion of the death of our lamented Chief Magistrate.*
>
> *Resolved, That this Hall be appropriately draped in mourning for 30 days, and that our citizens generally be requested to wear the usual badge of mourning for the like period.*[16]

The resolution was signed by H.R. Martin, clerk to the city council. Seven days later, it was noted in the April 24, 1865 minutes of the council that Lincoln's funeral cortege from Philadelphia passed through Rahway on its way to New York City at 8:25 a.m. A large emotional crowd showed up for the passage.

Soldiers returning to Rahway after the war joined one of the seven New Jersey Grand Army of the Republic (GAR) Posts, including the Rahway-based William F. Barry Post 27, which was active from July 23,

1879, to December 30, 1925. The names of twenty-five black Civil War veterans are listed on the 1893 membership roster. Edward M. Slater and Richard Stephens served as commanders of the post. Stephens was the last commander.

As a lasting tribute to its courageous soldiers, the Rahway-based Thomas Jardine and Son Monument Company was commissioned by the city to erect a Civil War monument at West Main and Irving Streets. The inscription reads: "To commemorate the valor of her sons who on land and sea fought in defence of the Union." The stone sculpture, a standing figure of a Union soldier, was dedicated on October 12, 1913.

Chapter 6

Union County Tribute to the Soldiers and Sailors

Over seventy-five Civil War veterans of African ancestry are buried at the historic Evergreen Cemetery, appropriately referred to as "an outdoor history book." The names of black soldiers and sailors carved into historic grave markers inscribed with the letters USCT for United States Colored Troops or USCI for United Sates Colored Infantry are material evidence of their service in the Civil War. Not so evident is that a significant number of the Civil War grave markers bear the name of blacks, who are not identified as such, who served in what has historically been assumed to be all-white regiments organized in Union County. The contributions of most of these soldiers came to light after extensive examination of Union County burial records at the Union County Office of Veteran Affairs in Elizabeth.

Evergreen Cemetery, incorporated March 23, 1853, set aside a section for Civil War veterans. In all, there are more than 1,500 veterans buried in the cemetery since the trustees set aside the veterans' area for free burials in 1862. The area is marked by two cannons obtained by Dr. William Mack, then mayor of Elizabeth, and dedicated on Memorial Day, May 30, 1900. The grave markers, some now well worn, stand in proud straight ranks. The Sixth Regiment United States Colored Troops, Re-enactors Inc., led by First Sergeant Fred Minus of Trenton, commemorated the contributions of USCT regiments during the Civil War at a ceremony held at the Evergreen Cemetery in October 2007.

Left: Civil War grave markers at Evergreen Cemetery, Hillside, New Jersey. *Courtesy Richard T. Koles.*

Below: The author *(third left)* with members of the Sixth Regiment United States Colored Troops, Re-enactors, Inc., at Evergreen Cemetery, Hillside. *Courtesy of the author.*

Civil War Soldier Monument erected in Elizabeth, New Jersey, circa 1906. *Courtesy Richard T. Koles.*

On June 10, 1865, Governor Joel Parker issued a proclamation to the people of New Jersey, urging each locality to plan special tributes to the brave soldiers of the Union on July 4, 1866, the date of the first anniversary of "our national independence." On May 30, 1906, almost forty years later, the Honorable Charles N. Fowler (1852–1932), a Republican Party politician who represented New Jersey's Eighth and Fifth Congressional districts in the United States House of Representatives, delivered the memorial address at the laying of the cornerstone of the Soldiers and Sailors Monument on Broad Street in Elizabeth, the county seat of government. A formal dedication of the granite sculpture was held on July 4, 1906.

Appendix A

Black Soldiers of Company B, Thirtieth New Jersey Infantry

There were four noncommissioned black officers of Company B, including Captain John N. Lewis, who resigned on December 27, 1862; First Lieutenant James S. Vanderveer; Second Lieutenant Thomas Moore, who resigned February 4, 1863; First Lieutenant John M. Case; and Corporal William G. Marsh, who was later reduced to rank of private. The reasons for the two resignations and reduction in rank could not be determined. The regiment was exposed to the Battle of Chancellorsville on May 2–3, 1863, but escaped the perils of actual combat. As noted below, a number of blacks had service in the United States Colored Troops (USCT) and/or the U.S. Navy and Marine Corps.

Name	Rank	Muster In	Muster Out	Bounty	Service
Eugene D. Badgley	wagoner	08.25.62	06.27.63		
John Beale	private	08.30.62	06.27.63		USCT
John B.W. Bennett	private	08.30.62	06.27.63	$100	USCT
Benjamin P. Bird	private	08.25.62	06.27.63	$100	USCT
Chetwood Bird	corporal	08.25.62			
	sergeant	04.01.63			
	first sergeant	05.12.63	06.27.63	$100	
William C. Boyle	private	08.25.62			
	corporal	10.07.62			
	sergeant	04.12.63	06.27.63		

Name	Rank	Muster In	Muster Out	Bounty	Service
John H. Brady	private	08.25.62	06.27.63		USCT
John Burns	private	08.25.62	06.27.63		USCT; U.S. Navy
William Carroll	private	08.30.62	06.27.63		USCT
John M. Case	first sergeant	08.25.62			
	second lieutenant	03.16.63			
	first lieutenant	05.09.63	06.27.63		USCT; U.S. Navy
William G. Casner	private	08.25.62			
	corporal	04.01.63	06.27.63		U.S. Navy
John F. Charleton	private	08.25.62	04.14.63		
Benjamin C. Clark	private	08.25.62	06.27.63		
Pembroeck S. Clark	private	08.25.62	06.27.63		
Samuel C. Clark	private	08.25.62	06.27.63	$100	USCT
James Connolly	private	08.25.62	06.27.63		USCT
Amos P. Cory	private	08.25.62	06.27.63		
George E. Dayton	private	08.25.62			
	sergeant major	09.18.62	06.27.63		
William H. DeHart	private	08.25.62			
	corporal	05.12.63	06.27.63	$100	U.S. Navy
Thomas Dennett	private	05.25.62			
	corporal	04.01.63			
	sergeant	05.16.63	06.27.63		
George W. Disbrow	private	08.25.62	06.27.63	$100	
John H. Doty	private	08.30.62	06.27.63		USCT
Horace F. Drake Jr.	private	08.25.62	06.27.63		
Jonathan B. Drake	private	08.26.62			
	hospital steward	09.18.62	06.27.63	$100	
William Durie	private	08.25.62			
	corporal	04.12.62	06.27.63		
Peter C. Fishbough	private	08.25.62	06.27.63		
Richard N. French	corporal	08.25.62			
	private	10.07.62	06.27.63		USCT

Name	Rank	Muster In	Muster Out	Bounty	Service
Henry Grogan	corporal	08.25.62	02.26.63 (deserted while on furlough)		
David A. Harrison	private	08.30.62	06.27.63		USCT
Samuel L. Hatfield	private	08.25.62	06.27.63		USCT
David B. Hetfield	private	08.25.62	06.27.63		
William E. Hoffman	private	08.30.62	06.27.63		USCT
William A. Jaques	private	08.25.62	04.09.63 (died of typhoid fever)		
Abram Jeroloman	corporal	08.25.62	06.27.63		USCT
Louis Keller	private	08.30.62	06.27.63		
John T. Kiggins	private	08.25.62	12.27.62 (died of fever)		USCT
Albert Lambert	private	08.25.62	06.27.63	$100	
John N. Lewis	captain	09.06.62	12.26.62 (resigned)		USCT
Thomas A. Little	corporal	08.25.62			
	sergeant	04.12.62	06.27.63		USCT
John Mahan	private	08.25.62			
	corporal	04.12.63	06.27.63	$100	USCT
William Marsh	private	08.25.62	06.27.63		USCT
William Griffin Marsh	private	08.30.62	06.27.63		
John Maxwell	private	08.25.62	06.27.63		
Theodore Meeker	private	08.25.62			
	corporal	10.07.62	06.27.63		
John P. Mendell	private	08.25.62	06.27.63		
William W. Mendell	private	08.25.62	06.27.63		
Henry C. Miller	private	08.30.62	06.27.63		USCT
Thomas Moore	second lieutenant	09.06.62	02.04.63 (resigned)		
Aaron W. Morgan	private	08.25.62	06.27.63		USCT
William M. Morse	private	08.25.62	06.27.63	$100	USCT
John K Mulford	private	08.25.62	06.27.63		
George E. Nash	private	08.30.62			
	corporal	10.07.62	06.27.63		USCT
Noah S. Noe	private	08.25.62	06.27.63		USCT

Name	Rank	Muster In	Muster Out	Bounty	Service
William C. Osburn	private	08.25.62	02.28.63 (died of typhoid fever)		
J. Abbott Parker	private	08.25.62	06.27.63		USCT
Robert W. Parsons	private	08.30.62	06.27.63		
Charles Peters	private	08.25.62	06.27.63		USCT
James Peterson	private	08.30.62	06.27.63		USCT
John H. Poole	private	08.25.62	06.27.63		USCT
George M. Price	private	08.25.62	06.27.63		USCT
John K. Rall	private	08.25.62	06.27.63	$100	
James H. Reeve	private	08.25.62	06.27.63		USCT
Julius A. Robinson	private	08.25.62	06.27.63		USCT
John R. Romain	private	08.25.62	06.27.63		USCT; U.S. Navy
Royal H. Rose	corporal	08.25.62			
	sergeant	04.12.63	06.27.63	$100	
George G. Rosendale	private	08.25.62	06.27.63		
John D. Ross	private	08.25.62	06.24.63 (died of disease)		USCT
David M. Ruckman	private	08.25.62	06.27.63		
Phineas G. Ruckman	private	08.25.62	06.27.63		
John S. Seabring	private	08.25.62	06.27.63		
John Sloan	private	08.25.62	06.27.63		USCT
George F. Smith	private	08.30.62	06.27.63		USCT
Isaac M. Stagg	private	08.25.62			
	first sergeant	04.01.63	05.12.63 (died)		
Edward P. Stansbury	private	08.25.62	04.17.63 (died of disease)		
George W. Taylor	private	08.25.62	06.27.63		USCT
Henry S. Ten Broeck	private	08.25.62	06.27.63		USCT
Jacob Thompson	private	08.25.62	06.27.63		USCT
William C. Toms	private	08.25.62	03.18.63 (discharged)		USCT
William F. Tooker	private	08.25.62			
	corporal	04.01.63			
	sergeant	05.12.63	06.27.63	$100	
Luther L. Valentine	corporal	08.25.62	03.12.63 (died)		

Black Soldiers of Company B, Thirtieth New Jersey Infantry

Name	Rank	Muster In	Muster Out	Bounty	Service
James S. Vandeveer	first lieutenant	12.26.62	06.27.63		USCT
Isaac van Hart	private	08.25.62	06.27.63		USCT
John J. van Houten	private	08.30.62	06.27.63		USCT
Washington O. Wilson	private	08.25.62	06.27.63		USCT
Willett H. Wood	private	08.25.62	06.27.63		USCT

Appendix B

United States Colored Troops

Official enrollment of blacks in the Union army began after President Lincoln issued the Emancipation Proclamation, which went into effect on January 1, 1863. The Bureau of Colored Troops was established by General Order 143 on May 22, 1863. All black troops were absorbed into the United States Colored Troops, or USCT, except for the Twenty-ninth Connecticut Infantry, the Fifty-fourth and Fifty-fifth Massachusetts Infantries and the Fifth Massachusetts Cavalry. Although New Jersey never organized any regiments of colored troops, most recruits were credited to the state. However, a significant number of recruits was credited to other states, including New York, Connecticut and Massachusetts.

Name	Birth–Death	Rank	Company	In–Out	Hometown or Burial Site	Miscellaneous
Simon Aaron	(1828–11.26.80)	sergeant	A 41st Infantry	09.03.64–09.30.65; recruit	Rahway Cemetery	$300 UC bounty
Henry Abrams	(1826–1907)	private	B 22nd Infantry	09.22.62–06.25.63	Baptist/Methodist Evergreen Cemetery; Plainfield	
William H. Ackerman	(1841–07.02.63)	private	A 22nd Infantry	09.01.62–06.25.63	Elizabeth; Gettysburg National Cemetery, Gettysburg, PA	killed 07.02.63 at Gettysburg
John B. Anderson	(1828–03.19.73)	first lieutenant	2nd Light Artillery, Battery B	04.10.64–07.12.65; recruit	Elizabeth; Evergreen Cemetery, Hillside	
Thomas B. Anderson	(1826–1886)	corporal	B 25th Infantry	12.28.64–12.06.65	Baptist/Methodist Evergreen Cemetery, Plainfield	Army Medal of Honor
George W. Ash	(d. 1914)	private	K 51st Mississippi Infantry	05.22.63–03.07.64	Elizabeth	
George B. Avery	(1843–12.10.1920)	private	D 40th Infantry	02.29.64	Hazelwood Cemetery, Rahway	
James H. Avery	(1825–1898)	private	96th Infantry	08.04.64	Rahway	$100 UC bounty
Richard H. Avery	(1843–10.04.1900)	corporal	K 116th Infantry	09.04.62–06.08.65		
		corporal		08.26.63		
		reduced to private		05.01.65	Rahway Cemetery (cremated)	
Simeon Avery	(d. 1880)	sergeant	A 41st Infantry	09.03.64–09.30.65; recruit	Rahway Cemetery	
Thomas Avery	(1847–05.04.72)	private	B 93rd Infantry	04.04.64–06.23.65	Hazelwood Cemetery, Rahway	
William H.H. Avery		captain	D 42nd Infantry	04.20.64–07.28.65; resigned	Rahway	$100 UC bounty

Name	Birth–Death	Rank	Company	In–Out	Hometown or Burial Site	Miscellaneous
John M. Baldwin	(d. 02.09.1902)	quartermaster	32nd Infantry	09.25.63–11.01.65		
		commanding captain	Company C, 32nd Infantry	10.24.65	Evergreen Cemetery, Hillside	
Isaac Ball		private	K 26th Infantry	09.18.62–06.27.63	Linden	
George Bauer	(d. 1864)	private	G 25th Infantry	09.26.62–06.20.63; drafted	Military Asylum Cemetery, Washington, D.C.	died of pneumonia at Washington, D.C.; $300 UC bounty
Henry Bauer		private	C 35th Infantry	02.25.64–07.20.65; substitute	Linden	
John Beale	(d. 12.27.1900)	private	D 68th Infantry	04.23.64–06.65	Rosedale Cemetery; Linden	
James Bean	(d. 03.31.80)	corporal	F 114th Infantry		Evergreen Cemetery, Hillside	
James Beatty		private	K 43rd Infantry	06.01.64–10.20.65	Elizabeth	
Henry Benjamin	(d. 6/19/65)	private	H 127th Infantry	09.01.64–09.07.65; recruit	Elizabeth	died of typhoid fever at Fort Barrancas, FL
John J. Bennett	(1838–1907)	private	G 1st Calvary	11.26.63–02.27.64	Evergreen Cemetery, Hillside	$100 UC bounty
Joseph R. Bennett	(1833–1900)	private	A 22nd Infantry	09.22.62–02.28.63	Rahway; Evergreen Cemetery, Hillside	
Charles Benson	(1839–1881)	private	D 65th Infantry	03.11.64–07.12.65	Plainfield	
Lewis Bergen	(1842–10.93)	corporal	H 127th Infantry	09.01.64–09.07.65	Elizabeth; Fairmount Cemetery, Newark, Essex County	
Henry Bias	(b. 1820)	private	D 13th Infantry	11.19.63–11.64		
Benjamin P. Bird	(1843–07.24.65)	private	I 127th Infantry	09.05.64–10.20.65	Vicksburg Cemetery, MS	died of chronic diarrhea; $300 bounty, 2nd Ward, Elizabeth; $100 UC bounty

Name	Birth–Death	Rank	Company	In–Out	Hometown or Burial Site	Miscellaneous
William Bishop		private	A 30th Infantry	09.09.64–12.20.65	Rahway	
George Blakins		private	H 127th Infantry	9.1.64–9.7.65	Elizabeth; Methodist Church Cemetery, Asbury, Warren County	
Henry F. Bolton		private	B 1st Regt. Calvary	8.15.61–6.20.62	Linden	
Henry Boyer	(1842–01.19.1911)	private	H 127thInfantry	09.01.64–09.07.65	New Somerville Cemetery, Somerville, Somerset County	
William Braden	(d. 01.17.90)	private	E 110th Infantry			
		private	A 67th Infantry Elizabeth		Old Public Grounds, Plot–Mt. 14, Evergreen Cemetery, Hillside	
John H. Brady	(1845–05.09.92)	private	C 63rd Infantry	12.21.64–01.09.66		
		promoted corporal		04.21.65	Plainfield	credited to Massachusetts
Henry C. Brandt	(1840–09.30.1912)	commissioned second lieutenant	I 25th Infantry	01.20.64–12.06.65	Elizabeth; Evergreen Cemetery, Hillside	
James H. Brandt	(d. 08.27.1906)	private	I 2nd District of Columbia		Hazelwood Cemetery, Rahway	
Isaac Brant	(1818)	private	E 7th Infantry	11.01.63–10.13.66		
		private	E 67th Infantry	02.13.64–07.12.65	Rahway	$300 Rahway bounty
Joseph Brant	(b. 1839)	corporal	E 104 Infantry	06.25.65–02.05.66	Elizabeth	
Robert Bray	(1840–04.05.94)	private	H 127th Infantry	08.31.64–09.07.65	Elizabeth; Evergreen Cemetery, Hillside	
William Bray	(1836–02.15.64)	private	E 5th Infantry	07.23.63–02.15.64	Elizabeth; Hampton National Cemetery, VA	died of disease in Norfolk, VA

Name	Birth–Death	Rank	Company	In–Out	Hometown or Burial Site	Miscellaneous
James Breen	(d. 03.31.80)	private	L 5th Massachusetts Colored Cavalry	04.22.64–12.16.64	Elizabeth; Old Public Grounds Division, Evergreen Cemetery, Hillside	wounded 06.15.64 at Baylor's Farm, VA
Michael Breen	(1846–01.13.1912)	assistant surgeon	8th Infantry	11.02.63–11.10.65	Fairview Cemetery, Westfield	
Boardman E. Brinkerhoff	(b. 1844)	private	E 25th Infantry	10.31.62–06.20.63	Plainfield	
George W. Brinkerhoff	(1839–1885)	corporal	A 22nd Infantry	09.22.62–06.25.63		
		promoted sergeant		03.11.63	Westfield	
John D. Brinkerhoff	(1830–10.24.1911)	private	I 22nd Infantry	09.22.62–06.25.63	Fairview Cemetery, Westfield	
Thomas Brokaw	(d. 09.08.65)	private	A 41st Infantry	09.05.64–09.08.65	Elizabeth; Section D, Grave 133, National Cemetery, Brownsville, TX	died at Edinburg, TX
Alexander Brown	(1832–04.30.1902)	private	A 26th Infantry	02.27.64–?	Hillside Cemetery, Scotch Plains	
Anson H. Brown	(b. 1845)	private	E 136th Infantry			
			A 104th Infantry		Rahway	$300 UC bounty
Clifford I. Brown	(d. 11.22.84)	private	C 74th Infantry		Evergreen Cemetery, Hillside	
George Henry Brown Jr.	(1842–04.11.65)	private	B 31st Infantry	02.22.64–04.11.65		died of consumption; $300 Rahway bounty
George Washington Brown	(1840–1902)	corporal	G 31st Infantry	08.09.64–11.07.65	Baptist/Methodist Evergreen Cemetery, Plainfield	

Name	Birth–Death	Rank	Company	In–Out	Hometown or Burial Site	Miscellaneous
James H. Brown	(1843–02.11.85)	private	K 22nd Infantry			
		corporal	F 31st Infantry	05.30.64–06.22.65		
		promoted corporal		01.01.65	Rahway; Evergreen Cemetery, Hillside	
Martin A. Brown	(1845–1905)	wagoner	29th Connecticut Infantry			
			F 51st Infantry	03.11.64	Fairview Cemetery, Westfield	
Milton A. Brown	(d. 11.30.64)	private	H 12th Heavy Artillery	09.13.64–11.30.64	Stones River National Cemetery, Murfreesboro, TN; removed to Fairview Cemetery, Westfield	killed at Franklin, TN
Theodore Brown	(b. 1841)	corporal	32nd Infantry	03.07.64–08.22.65		
		reduced to private		03.18.65	Plainfield	
Titus Clifford Brown	(1842–1884)	private	C 74th Infantry	04.4.64–10.11.65	Rahway; Evergreen Cemetery, Elizabeth	
William A. Brown		private	G 3rd Infantry	07.14.63–10.31.65	Westfield Presbyterian Churchyard Cemetery	
John Burns	(1842–04.15.97)	commissioned captain	C 48th Infantry	06.01.63–01.04.66		
		promoted captain	D 48th Infantry	12.06.63	St. Mary's Cemetery, Rahway	
John Carey	(1838–06.27.94)	private	H 25th Infantry	01.28.64–12.06.65	Elizabeth; Evergreen Cemetery, Hillside	
Prime Carmen	(1821–07.11.1902)	private	A 41st Infantry	09.02.64–09.30.65	Hillside Cemetery, Plainfield	

Name	Birth–Death	Rank	Company	In–Out	Hometown or Burial Site	Miscellaneous
David W. Carr	(b. 1830)	first lieutenant	F 6th Cavalry	08.20.63–09.15.65	Elizabeth	wounded at Petersburg, VA on 06.18.64; discharged for wounds on 05.17.65
Robert J. Carroll	(1844–01.21.1917)	private	I 25th Infantry	01.30.64–12.06.65	Elizabeth	
William Carroll	(1824–03.08.65)	sergeant	A 6th Infantry	07.28.63–03.08.65		
		reduced to private		05.30.64	Elizabeth; Mississippi River National Cemetery, Memphis, TN	
John T. Case	(1843–02.07.1912)	private	G 50th Infantry			
			D 68th Infantry	06.27.63 (mustered out)	Hillside Cemetery, Scotch Plains	
Edmond D. Chamberlain	(1842–06.21.91)	first sergeant	B 36th Infantry	10.12.64–06.8.65		
			reduced to rank of private		Fairview Cemetery, Westfield	
William Conner Chamberlain	(1843–07.06.1930	private	D 23rd Infantry	09.28.61–09.02.62	Hillside Cemetery, Scotch Plains	
John G. Champion	(d. 10.26.1906)	private	A 20th Infantry	02.09.64–10.07.65	Elizabeth, Evergreen Cemetery, Hillside	
William D. Chetwood	(1840–1922)				Evergreen Cemetery, Hillside	$300 3rd Ward bounty, Elizabeth
Amos Clark	(1808–1879)	private	D 52nd Infantry	09.01.63–05.05.66	Union	
David Brooks Clark	(1842–06.27.1906)	private	K 12th Heavy Artillery	07.21.64–07.15.65	Rahway Cemetery	
James R. Clark	(b. 1841)	private	A 22nd Infantry	09.22.62–06.25.63	Linden	

Name	Birth–Death	Rank	Company	In–Out	Hometown or Burial Site	Miscellaneous
Oliver Clark	(d. 04.15.1911)	private	I 63rd Infantry	12.14.63	Elizabeth	
Robert Clark	(07.06.18–09.09.62)	private	K 31st Infantry	09.09.62 (died)	Westfield Presbyterian Cemetery, Westfield	died of wounds received at Battle of Williamsburg
Samuel C. Clark	(1842–1898)	private	F 20th Infantry		Hazelwood Cemetery, Rahway	$100 UC bounty
Theodore C. Clark	(b. 1843)	lieutenant	1st Battalion of Cavalry, Mississippi Marine Brigade	02.63–08.64		
		second lieutenant	C 4th Cavalry 07.19.64			
		promoted first lieutenant		08.16.65	Rahway	
Thomas Clark	(1842–06.18.65)	private	E 27th Infantry	02.27.64–07.30.64	Rahway; Fairview Cemetery, Westfield	killed in action at Petersburg, VA
William H. Cleaveland	(1839–06.30.94)	private	G 8th Heavy Artillery	08.14.62–06.09.64	Evergreen Cemetery, Hillside	
Charles J. Clifford	(d. 03.02.1910)	private	D 22nd Infantry		Elizabeth; Evergreen Cemetery, Hillside	
James Clifford	(1844–1884)	private	D 22nd Infantry	12.14.63–01.11.65	Elizabeth; Chartiers Cemetery, Carnegie, PA	$100 UC bounty
Jabez C. Cole	(d. 04.06.1925)	private	I 52nd Infantry	09.23.61–06.01.62	Evergreen Cemetery, Hillside	
John A. Cole	(d. 06.16.1903)	sergeant	F 22nd Infantry	09.22.62–06.25.63	Evergreen Cemetery, Hillside	
Umewall Coles	(d. 1914)	private	C 25th Infantry		Baptist/Methodist Evergreen Cemetery, Plainfield	
James Connelly	(d. 04.30.1915)	private	C 37th Infantry		Mt. Olivet Cemetery, Elizabeth	$300 UC bounty
Samuel S. Conover	(1842–1891)	corporal	B 20th Infantry	02.9.64–08.10.65	Rahway Cemetery	

Name	Birth–Death	Rank	Company	In–Out	Hometown or Burial Site	Miscellaneous
William H. Conover	(1849–12.5.64)	private	A 22nd Infantry	12.03.63–12.05.64	Elizabeth	died at Fort Monroe, VA
John Conroy	(d. 02.10.95)	private	31st Infantry		Elizabeth; Evergreen Cemetery, Hillside	
Albert Cook	(d. 09.07.65)	private	A 41st Infantry	10.64–10.65	Rahway	died of typhoid fever at post hospital, Edinburg, TX
Charles Cook	(b. 1843)	corporal	D 20th Infantry			
			D 39th Infantry		Elizabethtown	
Cyrus E. Cook		sergeant	D 101st Infantry	10.64–07.65	Elizabeth	
Ellis L. Cook	(d. 02.03.1919)	private	K 68th Infantry	04.23.64–02.05.65	Elizabeth	
Henry H. Cook	(1841–01.29.1913)	private	K 20th Infantry	08.23.64–08.22.65	Elizabeth; Evergreen Cemetery, Hillside	
James Cook	(1811–06.28.70)	private	G 31st Infantry		Elizabeth; Evergreen Cemetery, Hillside	
William H. Cook	(1843–04.05.1914)	private	F 26th Infantry	02.27.64–01.02.65		
		Musician	B 22nd Infantry	12.24.63–10.16.65	Elizabeth; Evergreen Cemetery, Hillside	
John Corcoran	(1834–1898)	private	D 57th Infantry, E 6th Heavy Artillery		Elizabeth	
John T. Cox		corporal	I 25th Infantry	09.26.62–06.20.63		$300 UC bounty; Linden

Name	Birth–Death	Rank	Company	In–Out	Hometown or Burial Site	Miscellaneous
William H. Cox	(1841–1895)	private	C 31st Infantry	01.04.64–08.21.64	Hazelwood Cemetery, Rahway	$300 Rahway bounty, trained at Free Military School for Applicants for Command of Colored Troops. Rahway
Thomas Crane	(b. 1841)	private	E 11th Infantry		Elizabethtown	captured 06.09.63 at Brandy Station, VA; paroled 06.13.64 at City Point, VA
Oliver P. Cromwell	(b. 1843)	private	I 5th Regiment, Heavy Artillery		Elizabethtown	
Samuel S. Cromwell	(1837–06.28.64)	private	H 6th Infantry	09.01.63–06.28.64	Rahway	severely wounded in right leg (amputated) at Petersburg, VA on 06.18.64; died of wounds 06.28.64
Reverend David R. Croshon	(b. 02.15.34)	private	H 41st Infantry	05.02.64–09.03.64		$300 1st Ward bounty, Elizabeth
Jeremiah Crowell	(1830–1875)	private	5th Regiment, Heavy Artillery	03.11.64–07.12.65	Rahway Cemetery	
John Cuff	(d. 09.21.64)	private	C 25th Infantry	01.14.64–09.21.64		died at Fort Pickens, FL; $300 1st Ward, Elizabeth bounty
George T. Cummings		private	L 3rd Heavy Artillery		Elizabeth	discharged 02.15.64 at Brandy Station, VA for re-enlistment
William Dallas	(d. 03.27.1919)	private	F 28th Infantry	07.24.63–07.18.65	Fairview Cemetery, Westfield	

Name	Birth–Death	Rank	Company	In–Out	Hometown or Burial Site	Miscellaneous
Francis Davis	(d. 07.25.85)	private	C 22nd Infantry			
		corporal	A 6th Infantry	07.27.63–09.20.65	Elizabeth; Fairmount Cemetery, Newark, Essex County	
George O. Davis	(1841–02.03.95)	corporal	C 20th Infantry	02.09.64–10.07.65	Elizabeth; Evergreen Cemetery, Hillside	
Horace H. Davis		corporal	E 25th Infantry	09.18.62–06.20.63	Evergreen Cemetery, Hillside	
Samuel Davis		private	B 45th Infantry	06.04.64–11.04.65		$300 Springfield bounty
Daniel C. Day	(1844–06.23.1906)	private	D 43rd Infantry	08.04.64–10.20.65	Evergreen Cemetery, Hillside	
Horace H. Day	(1840–02.01.1918)	private	E 25th Infantry	09.18.62–01.12.63	Section L, Plot 30, Evergreen Cemetery, Hillside	
Nathaniel R. Day	(b. 1842)	private	K 6th Infantry	12.08.64–09.20.65		$300 Westfield bounty
Samuel E. Day		first lieutenant	C 31st Infantry			
			A 37th Infantry			
		first lieutenant	G 37th Infantry			
		commissioned captain		05.1864	Rahway	
William H. Day	(1847–09.08.1926)	private	K 9th Infantry	11.30.63–11.12.64	grave 59–d–5–8, Hillside Cemetery, Scotch Plains	
Henry W. De Camp	(b. 1841)	private	I 39th Infantry	1864–1865	Elizabeth	discharged for disability
William H. De Camp	(d. 07.04.1898)	engineer surgeon	1st Regiment, Michigan Colored Volunteers	02.17.64–09.30.65		

Name	Birth–Death	Rank	Company	In–Out	Hometown or Burial Site	Miscellaneous
Charles R. DeGraw	(1831–1898)	private	A 22nd Infantry	09.22.62–06.25.63	Elizabeth; Colonel Ledyard Cemetery, Groton, CT	
John DeGraw	(d. 1881)	private	K 25th Infantry		Section G, Plot 53–54, Hazelwood Cemetery, Rahway	
John W. De Hart	(1841–05.20.73)	private	B 41st Infantry	10.03.64–10.18.65		
			transferred from Company G		Elizabeth; Evergreen Cemetery, Hillside	
William Deyo		private	A 20th Infantry	02.09.64–10.07.65	Plainfield	
Charles Dickerson	(d. 06.18.64)	corporal	A 41st Infantry	09.03.64–09.30.65	Rahway Cemetery	killed in Battle in Front of Petersburg
William A. Dickerson	(1829–1880)				Rahway hometown	
Theodore Disbrow	(1843–04.15.63)	private	E 54th Massachusetts Infantry	03.29.63–04.15.63	Rahway	died of disease at Readville, MA, before muster
Thomas Ditmars	(1838–03.08.83)		unassigned USCT		Evergreen Cemetery, Hillside	
John H. Doty	(1844–01.04.1937)	private	K 12th Heavy Artillery	Elizabeth		
Robert J. Douglass		private	11th Infantry			discharged at Ward General Hospital, Newark, NJ
George W. Drake	(1842–06.07.65)	lieutenant	B 108th Infantry			
			G 58th Mississippi Infantry (African Descent)		Evergreen Cemetery, Hillside	died of fever on board USS *Arkansas* at Pensacola, FL

Name	Birth–Death	Rank	Company	In–Out	Hometown or Burial Site	Miscellaneous
Mark L. Drake		private	G 43rd Infantry	04.13.64–10.20.65		
		promoted sergeant		05.05.65	Elizabeth	$300 UC bounty
Noah W. Drake	(1836–09.25.1911)	private	B 73rd Illinois Infantry			
			B 44th Illinois Infantry		10.04.64–06.12.65	Division 8, Section A, Soldiers Plot, Grave 17, Hillside Cemetery, Scotch Plains
Burton Drew	(11.09.1913)	second lieutenant	I 38th Infantry	03.03.65-01.25.67		
		promoted first lieutenant	Company D	08.28.66	Rosedale Cemetery, Linden	
Edward M. Dubois	(b. 1836)	private	B 14th Regiment, Rhode Island Colored Heavy Artillery	09.14.63–01.07.65	Elizabeth	discharged for disability at Fort Jackson, LA
Joseph Dunham	(d. 01.26.1925)	private	E 29th Connecticut Infantry		Hillside Cemetery, Scotch Plains	wounded 09.30.64 at Richmond, VA
William H. Dunham	(1838–01.12.91)	captain	36th Infantry	09.06.64	Rahway; Section M, Plot 418, Rahway Cemetery	discharged at USA Hospital, West Philadelphia, PA, for wounds received at Cold Harbor, VA; $100 UC bounty
David J. Dunn		private	C 120th Infantry	02.01.64–06.21.65	Rahway	

Name	Birth–Death	Rank	Company	In–Out	Hometown or Burial Site	Miscellaneous
William H. Dunn	(1848–06.30.1900)	private	H 127th Infantry	09.01.64–10.25.65	Trinity Churchyard, Woodbridge	$300 1st Ward, Elizabeth bounty
John H. Edgar	(1825–05.29.99)	private	A 41st Infantry	09.03.64–09.30.65	Strangers section, Rahway Cemetery	
Mahlon Edgar	(1840–10.17.1915)	private	C 3rd Infantry	07.03.63–10.31.65	Rahway Cemetery	
William A. Edgerton	(1833–07.30.1880)	second lieutenant	E 13th Heavy Artillery	04.18.65–11.18.65	Elizabeth; Evergreen Cemetery, Hillside	
Joseph H. Edwards	(b. 1826)	private	B 31st Infantry	08.10.63–05.24.65	Elizabeth; Fairview Cemetery, Westfield	
Thomas Ellis	(b. 1841)	private	2nd Light Artillery, Battery A		Rahway	
John Henry Elson	(1831–02.12.1914)	private	K 31st Infantry	09.17.62–06.24.63	Evergreen Cemetery, Hillside	
Edward M. Esterbrooks	(1838–12.24.1903)	private	1st Massachusetts Cavalry	12.27.64–06.30.65	Section A, Plot 126, Grave 3, Evergreen Cemetery, Hillside	wounded at Gettysburg, PA, 07.02.63
David J. Farmer	(d. 05.05.99)	private	A 127th Infantry	08.22.64–05.29.65	Evergreen Cemetery, Hillside	
Benjamin Ferguson	(1841–01.16.64)	private	C 22nd Infantry		Rahway; Lebanon Cemetery, Philadelphia, PA	
James W. Fisher	(1843–03.12.81)	private	E 22nd Infantry	12.24.63–04.30.65	British Honduras (Belize); Elizabeth; Evergreen Cemetery, Hillside	wounded at Chaffin's Farm, VA, 09.29.64; discharged for wounds

Name	Birth–Death	Rank	Company	In–Out	Hometown or Burial Site	Miscellaneous
George C. Ford		private	A 3rd Regiment Cavalry			
			unassigned infantry	05.23.64–10.02.64	Linden	
Charles L. Francis	(1839–02.03.65)	private	K 20th Infantry	02.09.64–02.03.65	Elizabeth; Evergreen Cemetery, Hillside	died at Carrolton, LA
Edward Francis	(d. 1870)	corporal	A 41 Infantry	09.10.64–09.30.65	Elizabeth; Evergreen Cemetery, Hillside	
Elias Francis	(1845–05.21.1917)	private	D 20th Infantry	02.09.64–10.07.65	Elizabeth; Evergreen Cemetery, Hillside	
John Frederick	(1814–1883)	coal heaver	I 8th Infantry	09.03.64–12.27.64		
			H 52nd Infantry			
			I 56th Infantry		Elizabeth; Linden	
Albert T. Freeman	(1844–11.10.83)		M 1st Cavalry; G 27th Infantry	08.16.64–09.21.65	Rahway	wounded and captured in action 06.09.63 at Brandy Station, VA; paroled 12.02.64 at City Point, VA
Charles P. Freeman	(1841–06.08.1914)	private	B 39th Infantry	09.30.64–06.17.65		
		corporal		10.09.64	Section J, Plot 591, Rahway Cemetery	
Enos E. Freeman	(1826–01.14.79)	corporal	H 22nd Infantry	01.02.64–10.16.65	Rahway Cemetery	
Joseph M. Freeman	(1843–08.14.64)	private	H 22nd Infantry	01.02.64		
		corporal	B 108th Infantry	06.15.64	Rahway Cemetery	died at U.S. Army Hospital, Fortress Monroe, VA

Name	Birth–Death	Rank	Company	In–Out	Hometown or Burial Site	Miscellaneous
Samuel W. Freeman		private	C 28th Infantry	07.02.64–11.08.65	Rahway	
Richard N. French		private	G 31st Infantry	C 13th Infantry	Elizabeth	
James Fulton	(b. 1837)	sergeant	A 22nd Infantry	09.22.62–06.25.63		
		drummer	C 10th Heavy Artillery		Rahway	
David S. Giles		private	88th Infantry (New Tennessee Organization)			wounded at Walthall, VA 05.06.64
William H. Gill	(d.12.16.1882)	corporal	F 22nd Infantry		Elizabeth; Mt. Olivet Cemetery, Elizabeth	
William Godfrey	(d. 07.07.92)	private	K 27 Infantry	01.26.64–06.16.65	Elizabeth; Evergreen Cemetery, Hillside	
Samuel Godshalk	(d. 05.23.1907)	private	B 104th Infantry			
		corporal		05.09.62		
		reduced to private		01.05.63	Section H, Row 1, Block 26, Grave 2, Fairview Cemetery, Westfield	
John H. Good	(1843–10.23.1927)	private	G 25th Infantry	01.26.64–12.06.65	Elizabeth; Evergreen Cemetery, Hillside	
George Goodwin	(1821–03.19.64)	private	D 6th Infantry	07.13.63–03.19.64	Fairview Cemetery, Westfield	died at Yorktown, VA
William J. Gould	(b. 1843)	private	A 41st Infantry	09.05.64–09.30.65		
			K 22nd Infantry	04.03.65–10.16.65	Rahway	
Robert Graham	(1823–11.01.99)	corporal	I 8th Infantry		Linden; Evergreen Cemetery, Hillside	
Halsey B. Green		second lieutenant	E 91st Infantry	09.01.63–07.07.64	Plainfield	

Name	Birth–Death	Rank	Company	In–Out	Hometown or Burial Site	Miscellaneous
James W. Green	(d. 04.20.65)	private	G 22nd Infantry	07.12.65 (mustered out)	Cypress Hill Cemetery, Brooklyn, NY	
John H. Green	(d. 03.24.1903)	private	G 29th Connecticut Infantry	03.08.64-10.24.65		
		promoted corporal		?–03.01.65	Evergreen Cemetery, Hillside	
Samuel K. Green	(1845–03.05.99)	private	C 25th Infantry			
		private	K 22nd Infantry	01.04.64–07.26.64	Hillside Cemetery, Scotch Plains	wounded in action, 07.26.64
John Gregory			F 23rd Infantry			
		field and staff surgeon	15th Infantry			
		corporal	B 35th Infantry			
		promoted sergeant			Linden	
Anthony Hall	(1845–08.29.1907)	private	B 25th Infantry	10.22.64–12.06.65	Elizabeth; Evergreen Cemetery, Hillside	
George B. Hall	(1845–10.15.1917)	musician	Battery E 11th U.S. Colored Heavy Artillery		Evergreen Cemetery, Hillside	
James Hall	(1840–09.20.84)	private	E 39th Infantry			
		corporal	C 8th Infantry			
			F 25th Infantry	01.03.65–12.06.65	Old Public Grounds, Evergreen Cemetery, Hillside	

Name	Birth–Death	Rank	Company	In–Out	Hometown or Burial Site	Miscellaneous
Enoch W. Hand	(b. 1839)	private	E 25th Infantry	09.18.62–06.20.63		
			K 2nd Michigan Infantry	04.14.64–03.04.65	Plainfield	wounded at Battle of Kinston, NC, 12.14.62 by a musket ball; discharged for wounds, 07.28.65
Henry Wells Hand	(1841–1905)	captain	I 39th Infantry	04.18.64–12.04.65	Scotch Plains Baptist Church Cemetery	trained at Free Military School for Applicants for Commands of Colored Troops, Philadelphia
David A. Harrison		private	K 43rd Infantry	05.30.64–10.20.65	Elizabeth	
John H. Harrison	(b. 1826)	private	C 20th Infantry	02.09.64–10.07.65		
			I 8th Infantry	11.10.63–11.10.65	Port Elizabeth	
John H. Hart	(1845–07.15.1864)	private	B 31st Infantry	02.01.64–02.09.64	Elizabeth	
John Harvey		private	B 6th Infantry	07.13.63–09.20.65	Rahway	
Samuel L. Hatfield	(1842–1897)	private	E 127th Infantry	08.23.64–10.20.65	Linden	
Charles R. Hawkins	(1846–08.20.1924)	private	K 3rd Infantry	12.20.64–10.31.65	Evergreen Cemetery, Hillside	
Abram Henry	(1831–11.17.1907)	corporal	A 25th Infantry	01.13.64–12.06.65	Baptist/Evergreen Methodist Cemetery, Plainfield	
George W. Henry	(b. 1843)	private	B 43rd Infantry	02.26.64–10.20.65	Plainfield	
Henry Henry	(1830–1880)	private	B 43rd Infantry	03.15.64–10.20.65	Elizabeth	$300 UC bounty
Thomas Henry	(1832–1883)	private	B 3rd Infantry	06.30.63		
		private	H 22nd Infantry	10.01.64–10.16.65	Elizabeth	$250 UC bounty

Name	Birth–Death	Rank	Company	In–Out	Hometown or Burial Site	Miscellaneous
William Henry	(1842–04.26.1906)	private	E 6th Infantry	08.20.63–09.20.65	Elizabeth; Evergreen Cemetery, Hillside	$100 UC bounty
Martin Herling	(1841–11.13.1907)	private	A 41st Infantry	09.02.64–09.30.65	Division 8, Section A, Soldiers Plot, Grave 13, Hillside Cemetery, Scotch Plains	
David S.C. Higgins Jr.	(1843–1865)	private	B 41st Infantry	09.09.64–10.13.64	Union; Evergreen Cemetery, Hillside	
Thomas Higgins	(1824–11.18.95)	private	H 22nd Infantry	09.22.62–06.25.63	Block B, Mt. Olivet Cemetery, Elizabeth	
William E. Hill	(1838–02.01.1913)	corporal	G 25th Infantry	01.27.64–12.06.65	Elizabeth; Evergreen Cemetery, Hillside	
John Hoff	(d. 1905)	sergeant	A 31st Infantry		Division 23, Oak Drive Section, Plot 20, Presbyterian Cemetery, Springfield	
Abraham Holland	(d. 12.16.64)	captain	A 32nd Infantry	12.16.64	Beauford Cemetery, SC	$100 UC bounty
George L. Holland	(1842–1909)		L 1st Cavalry	10.07.64–07.24.65		
			D 1st Cavalry		Fairview Cemetery, Westfield	
John C. Holland	(b. 1846)	commissioned captain	3rd Louisiana Native Guard	02.19.63 (resigned for reason of prejudice)		
		private	F 25th Infantry	01.26.64–02.17.64		
		private	F 32nd Infantry	02.26.64–08.22.65	Fairview Cemetery, Westfield	
Jacob P.J. Howard	(b. 1838)	private	C 83rd Infantry	08.17.63–07.28.64		
		private	K 45th Infantry	02.22.64–06.15.65	Rahway	prisoner of war at Poplar Springs Church, VA, 09.30.64

Name	Birth–Death	Rank	Company	In–Out	Hometown or Burial Site	Miscellaneous
Samuel Howard		private	127th Infantry	08.16.64–10.20.65		
		private	A 6th Infantry	07.25.63–04.26.64	Linden; Mount Moriah Cemetery, Hainesport, Burlington County	discharged by special order
James Frank Hubbard	(d. 03.07.1905)	private	B 25th Infantry	01.15.64–04.24.64	Hillside Cemetery, Scotch Plains	
Thomas R. Hunt		private	6th Heavy Artillery	09.10.62–05.02.63		
		chaplain	2nd Light Artillery, Battery A	05.31.64–08.17.64	Rahway	wounded in action at Chancellorsville, VA
James H. Ingraham	(b. 1838)	commissioned first lieutenant	I 73rd Infantry	10.01.62		
		recommended for promotion captain	1st Louisiana Native Guard	10.63–3.22.64	Rahway	captured 06.09.63 at Brandy Station, VA; paroled 06.13.63 at City Point; resigned for reason of prejudice 03.22.64
George Jackson	(1820–03.16.99)	private	A 41st Infantry	09.05.64–09.30.65	Rahway Cemetery.	slave prior to April 9, 1861; $300 Rahway bounty
George W. Jackson	(1844–1905)	private	B 25th Infantry	01.07.64–06.14.64		
			G 41st Infantry	09.19.64–09.30.65	Rahway Cemetery.	
Henry L. Jackson	(1843–02.18.1926)	private	B 20th Infantry	12.21.63–10.07.65	plot 172, Evergreen Cemetery, Hillside	
John K. Jackson		private	A 22nd Infantry	01.08.64–04.11.65		

Name	Birth–Death	Rank	Company	In–Out	Hometown or Burial Site	Miscellaneous
Richard Jackson	(1843–06.06.1907)	private	C 45th Infantry	05.12.64–12.15.65	Linden; Memorial Park Cemetery, Gouldtown, Cumberland County	
Thomas H. Jackson	(1834–09.19.1910)	musician	I 45th Infantry	08.11.64–11.04.65	Evergreen Cemetery, Hillside	
Thomas R. Jackson	(1818–07.03.97)	private	A 41st Infantry	09.03.64–09.30.65	Rahway Cemetery	
William H. Jackson	(1835–04.25.1916)	private	G 29th Connecticut Infantry		Rahway Cemetery	
David B. Jenkins	(1840–03.10.81)	sergeant	K 39th Infantry	03.03.62–09.10.63 (detached on recruiting service at New Orleans June 1863)		
		commissioned captain	Corps d'Afrique	09.10.63–12.30.64		
		captain	K 86th Infantry		Evergreen Cemetery, Hillside	
John Johnson	(d. 02.07.64)	private	F 22nd Infantry		Presbyterian Cemetery, New Providence	
John H. Johnson	(1840–07.13.63)	private	E 39th Infantry		Rahway Cemetery	missing in action at Gettysburg, PA, 07.03.63, presumed dead
John L. Johnson	(1844–05.09.83)	private	B 3rd Infantry	01.17.65–10.31.65	Elizabeth	$250 UC bounty
William D. Johnson	(1844–05.22.1908)	private	H 20th Infantry	12.14.63–10.07.65		
			I 8th Infantry	11.03.63–11.10.65	Scotch Plains Baptist Church Cemetery, Scotch Plains	

Name	Birth–Death	Rank	Company	In–Out	Hometown or Burial Site	Miscellaneous
Albert G. Jones	(1841–1875)	commissioned corporal	B 27th Infantry	01.19.64–04.22.65		
		second lieutenant		01.19.64		
		first lieutenant and adjutant		09.10.64	Rahway Cemetery	
Frank J. Jones	(b. 1838)	commissioned second lieutenant	L Connecticut 1st Light Artillery	03.13.62–07.27.63		
		promoted first lieutenant		0.1.01.63	Rahway	
Henry Jones	(1837–05.09.87)	sergeant	E 103rd Infantry	03.10.65–04.15.66		
		corporal	H 127th Infantry	09.01.64	Jamaica; Evergreen Cemetery, Hillside	
Samuel Kellum	(1825–11.02.1908)	corporal	K 36th Infantry	01.13.64–12.06.65	Rosehill Cemetery, Linden	
Daniel Kennedy		private	H 2nd Infantry	10.01.64–03.21.66		
Francis Kennedy	(d. 04.03.1924)	private	4th Brigade, 3rd Division, 2nd Army Corps	05.64–07.64	Section Wilbur, Plot 217, Grave 3, Rosedale Cemetery, Linden	
John T. Kiggins	(d. 12.27.62)	private	I 49th Infantry		Evergreen Cemetery, Hillside	died of fever at Aquia Creek, VA
Joseph H. King	(1845–07.31.64)	private	I 20th Infantry	02.09.64–07.31.64	Rahway	died at Carrolton, LA
William N. King	(1841–1926)	private	B 40th Infantry	01.06.65–07.13.65	Elizabeth; Evergreen Cemetery, Hillside	
William Baker Kinsey		first lieutenant	A 111th Infantry	02.14.65	Linden	

Name	Birth–Death	Rank	Company	In–Out	Hometown or Burial Site	Miscellaneous
Robert Lane		private	D 41st Infantry	09.17.64–09.30.65	Westfield	
Theodore Latin		private	H 127th Infantry	08.31.64–09.07.65	Elizabeth	
Charles P. Layton	(1846–10.19.64)	private	C 20th Infantry	10.19.64	Section G, single grave, Baptist/ Methodist Evergreen Cemetery, Plainfield	killed in action at Cedar Creek, VA governmental burial 02.09.1916
Samuel Layton	(d. 12.10.99)	private	M 2nd Cavalry	08.16.64–06.29.65	Section 10, Plot 14, Baptist/ Methodist Evergreen Cemetery, Plainfield	
Peter Lee	(d. 1902)	private	F 22nd Infantry	12.29.63–10.16.65	Elizabeth	$250 UC bounty UC; former slave, freed by law of 1804
William Lee	(1841–01.31.1903)	corporal	E 64th Infantry	01.01.64	Elizabeth; Evergreen Cemetery, Hillside	$100 UC bounty
Henry H. Leeds	(d. 08.21.1915)	private	6th Cavalry	11.12.64	Evergreen Cemetery, Hillside	
Charles H. Leonard	(b. 1842)	sergeant	I 20th Infantry		Rahway	
Anderson Lewis	(1847–03.21.1915)	private	B 11 Infantry			
			G 113th Arkansas Infantry			
			C 43rd Infantry		Section L, Grave 20, Rahway Cemetery	
John N. Lewis	(b. 1843)	private	A 31st Infantry	04.29.64–07.08.64		
			D 25th Infantry	01.16.64–12.06.65	Elizabeth	
Isaiah Lineman	(1839–1916)	corporal	D 41st Infantry	09.21.64–09.30.65	Baptist/Methodist Evergreen Cemetery, Plainfield	
Henry A. Little		private	B 4th Heavy Artillery	03.17.64–12.11.65		$300 UC bounty; Westfield

Name	Birth–Death	Rank	Company	In–Out	Hometown or Burial Site	Miscellaneous
Jacob Little	(d. 06.01.64)	private	G 25th Infantry	09.26.62–06.20.63	National Cemetery, Cold Harbor, VA	killed at Cold Harbor, VA
James A. Little	(d. 12.27.1924)	sergeant	F 19th Infantry		Evergreen Cemetery, Hillside	
Thomas A. Little	(1831–03.09.1907)	corporal	F 57th Infantry			
			I 52nd Infantry		Elizabeth; Hillside Section, Plot 456, Grave 1 & 2, Rosedale Cemetery, Linden	
John Mackey	(d. 08.14.1912)	private	A 45th Infantry	06.13.64–11.04.65	Hillside Cemetery, Scotch Plains	
John Mahan	(d. 01.05.64)	private	D 31st Infantry		Military Asylum Cemetery, Washington, D.C.	$100 UC bounty
James Malson		sergeant	B 41st Infantry	09.05.64–09.30.65	Elizabeth	
Daniel Manning	(d. 06.20.1913)	private	A 41st Infantry	09.03.64–09.30.65	Plainfield; Fairview Cemetery, Westfield	
Henry S. Manning	(1834–09.08.1910)	second lieutenant	B 82nd Infantry		Hazelwood Cemetery, Rahway	
Charles G. Marsh	(1844–01.12.1921)	first lieutenant	E 25th Infantry	12.30.62–06.20.63	Elizabeth; Evergreen Cemetery, Hillside	$300 Westfield bounty
Peter Marsh	(d. 10.20.64)	private	E 6th Infantry	08.16.63–10.20.64	Westfield; National Cemetery, Hampton, VA	
Robert Marsh	(1844–05.26.1914)	corporal	D 20th Infantry		Hillside Cemetery, Scotch Plains	
William G. Marsh	(1825–06.01.80)	private	C 61st Infantry	08.08.63		
			C 110th Infantry	01.1.64	Methodist Cemetery, New Providence	
William M. Marsh	(1837–1934)	private	I 8th Infantry	11.12.63–11.10.65	Rahway Cemetery	$300 Rahway bounty; $100 UC bounty

Name	Birth–Death	Rank	Company	In–Out	Hometown or Burial Site	Miscellaneous
John V. Martin	(d. 11.26.1898)	private	B 25th Infantry	10.31.62–06.20.63	Elizabeth; Section E, Plot 113, Grave 3–rear, Evergreen Cemetery, Hillside	
Henry T. Maxwell		private	A 43rd Infantry	02.26.64–10.20.65	Elizabeth	
Reverend Thomas C. Mayham	(1841–11.08.1915)	private	4th Heavy Artillery		Lawncrest A, Plot 333, Grave 2–Front, Evergreen Cemetery, Hillside	
Edwin Maynard	(d. 10.05.1909)				Hillside Cemetery, Scotch Plains	
Robert McCandless	(1817–1845)	private	F 23rd Infantry	02.24.65–02.24.68	Elizabeth; Evergreen Cemetery, Hillside	
Samuel W. McDonald	(b. 1832)	quartermaster sergeant	6th Heavy Artillery			
		sergeant No. 6 Gun	D 11th Infantry	09.01.63–06.21.64	Rahway	
Henry McFarland		private	G 61st Infantry			
			K 62nd Infantry		Rahway	
James McKinney	(d. 01.26.1886)	private	F 25th Infantry	02.28.65–12.06.65	Section D, Soldiers Plot 87, Grave 82, Evergreen Cemetery, Hillside	
Samuel L. McKinney	(1840–06.11.1890)	private	F 25thInfantry	02.28.65–12.06.65		
			H 107th Infantry		Rahway; Strangers Section, Grave 148, Rahway Cemetery	
Charles Middlesworth	(d. 12.30.1907)	private	F 22nd Infantry	01.11.63–10.16.65	Rahway Cemetery	
Enoch Milford	(1833–09.11.1918)	private	F 25th Infantry	01.25.64–12.06.65	Hillside Cemetery, Scotch Plains	
Henry C. Miller	(d. 08.27.1915)	private	F 101st Infantry		Evergreen Cemetery, Hillside	

Name	Birth–Death	Rank	Company	In–Out	Hometown or Burial Site	Miscellaneous
John L. Miller	(d. 01.30.1917)	private	D 25th Infantry	01.18.64–12.06.65		
		private	B 31st Infantry	04.14.64–11.07.65	Fairview Cemetery, Westfield	
Joseph W. Miller		**private**	**K 26th Infantry**		**Elizabeth**	
Owens Miller		private	F 22nd Infantry	12.29.63–01.28.64	Elizabeth	$250 UC bounty
James W. Mitchell	**(1825-11.07.1881)**	**private**	**G 27th Infantry**	**08.15.64–09.04.65**	**Division 5, Section C, Row 7, Colored Adult, Grave 21, Hillside Cemetery, Scotch Plains**	
George W. Moore	(b. 5.6.1840)	corporal	A 22nd Infantry	12.21.63–10.16.65	Hazelwood Cemetery, Rahway	
Reverend Samuel T. Moore	**(1844–11.21.1905)**	**chaplain**	**K 8th Infantry**	**10.12.64–07.17.65**	**Hillside Cemetery, Scotch Plains**	
Aaron W. Morgan		private	H 119th Infantry			
Joseph M. Morris	**(1844–08.05.64)**	**private**	**H 20th Infantry**	**02.09.64–08.05.64**	**Linden**	**died at Corps d' Afrique Hospital, New Orleans from wounds received in action**
Albert Morse		private	E 65th Infantry	08.24.64–06.12.65	Linden	
John R. Morse	**(d. 1896)**	**private**	**D 25 Infantry**	**01.19.64–12.06.65**	**Hazelwood Cemetery, Rahway**	
Joseph E. Morse Jr.	(d. 02.11.1921)	private	K 39th Infantry	09.23.64–06.17.65	Hillside Cemetery, Scotch Plains	
Robert Morse	**(1818–10.05.1899)**	**private**	**D 25th Infantry**	**03.02.65–12.06.65**	**Hazelwood Cemetery, Rahway**	
William M. Morse	(02.15.1911)	private	K 8th Heavy Artillery	06.25.64		
			E 3rd Cavalry	08.30.64–06.06.65		
		private	E 25th Infantry	09.18.62–06.20.63	Linden; Evergreen Cemetery, Hillside	$100 UC bounty
George W. Mulford		**private**	**C 32nd Infantry**	**02.27.64–08.27.65**	**Linden**	

Name	Birth–Death	Rank	Company	In–Out	Hometown or Burial Site	Miscellaneous
Charles Mulligan		private	E 26th Infantry	09.18.62–06.27.63	Linden	
James Rankin Mullikin	(d. 03.08.1922)	first lieutenant	K 25th Infantry	03.18.64–12.07.65		
			97th Infantry	12.07.65–04.30.66	Evergreen Cemetery, Hillside	wounded in action
Samuel Murray	(d. 03.24.1901)	private	B 25th Infantry	02.11.65–12.06.65		
			E 19th Infantry	01.05.64–04.17.64	Evergreen Cemetery, Hillside	
Thomas Murray	(d. 05.28.1863)	private	F 41st Infantry		Elizabeth; Military Asylum Cemetery, Washington, D.C.	died at U.S. Army General Hospital, Washington, D.C., of wounds received in action at Chancellorsville, VA
George E. Nash		private	H 28th Infantry	08.03.64–08.15.64		
		musician	E 26th Infantry		Elizabeth	
John H.C. Nelson	(b. 1841)	sergeant	C 26th Infantry	09.18.62–06.27.63		
			K 43rd Infantry	05.28.64–10.20.65	Westfield	trained at Free Military School for Applicants for Commands of Colored Troops, Philadelphia
William H. Newbern	(d. 06.08.65)	musician	D 60th Infantry		Elizabeth	died at Finley U.S. Army General Hospital, Washington, D.C.
Noah S. Noe	(1830–09.12.1901)	corporal	G 37th Infantry	06.23.64–10.01.64	Linden; Rahway Cemetery	$300 UC bounty
Smith H. Noe	(1820–1889)	private	C 12th Infantry		Rahway Cemetery	$300 UC bounty

Name	Birth–Death	Rank	Company	In–Out	Hometown or Burial Site	Miscellaneous
Robert Obe		corporal	F 22nd Infantry	12.29.63–10.16.65	Elizabeth	$250 UC bounty
Charles R. Oliver	(1843–07.03.1906)	color sergeant	G 43rd Infantry 02.03.64		Section J, Oliver Vault, Rahway Cemetery	wounded 06.08.63 at Brandy Station
James H. Oliver	(b. 1845)	private	I 5th Massachusetts Colored Cavalry	12.24.64–06.12.65	Evergreen Cemetery, Hillside; Elizabeth	$100 UC bounty
Samuel M. Oliver	(d. 01.24.1905)	private	I 2nd Infantry	02.29.64–09.12.65	Section J, Outside Oliver Vault, Rahway Cemetery	
William H. Oliver		private		08.31.64–09.07.65	Rahway	
William H. Olmstead	(b. 1839)	private	F 5th Infantry	08.17.64–08.29.65	Rahway	
William N. Pangborn	(d. 06.27.1927)	first lieutenant	I 63rd Infantry		Hillside Cemetery, Scotch Plains	
Edward C. Parker	(b. 1843)	private	31st Infantry	05.06.64	Linden	
James E. Parker	(b. 1842)	first lieutenant	K 12th Heavy Artillery	08.02.64		
			D 19th Infantry	05.19.64–01.15.67	Rahway Cemetery	
John A. Parker	(b.1844)	private	A 25th Infantry			
			G 20th Infantry	02.09.64–10.07.65	Elizabeth	
William H. Patterson		private	D 43rd Infantry	03.26.64–10.20.65	Rahway	$300 UC bounty
William Pease	(1842–12.23.64)	private	A 2nd Cavalry	12.15.63–01.250.64	Elizabeth	
Nathan C. Pennington	(d. 11.22.1919)	private	C 28th Infantry	09.22.62–07.06.63	Division 4, Section A, Plot 127, Hillside Cemetery, Scotch Plains	
Samuel W. Pennington	(d. 06.26.64)	private	H 6th Infantry	09.07.63–06.26.64	Rahway; Row 20, Section E, Grave 30, National Cemetery, Hampton, VA	died of disease at Fort Monroe

Name	Birth–Death	Rank	Company	In–Out	Hometown or Burial Site	Miscellaneous
John Perkins		private	C 8th Infantry	09.21.63 11.10.65	Linden	
Albert G. Perry		captain	K 95th Infantry	04.28.63–11.26.64	Plainfield	
Charles Peters		corporal	I 6th Infantry	08.12.63–09.20.65	Elizabeth	
George Peters	(1823–01.25.83)	private	K 31st Infantry	12.31.64–11.07.65	Elizabeth; Section A, Map 3, Plot 33, Grave 3–Front, Evergreen Cemetery, Hillside	
James P. Phillips	(d. 05.05.62)	sergeant	K 118th Infantry		Rahway	killed in action at Williamsburg, VA
Elijah Pippenger	(1825–05.17.95)	private	F 25th Infantry	03.04.65–12.06.65	Rahway Cemetery	$300 Rahway bounty
John H. Poole		private	C 11th Heavy Artillery			
Joseph H. Post	(1838–06.01.63)	first lieutenant	A 22nd Infantry	09.22.62–02.28.63		
		promoted adjutant		01.1.63	Elizabethtown	died of typhoid fever at Camp near White Oak Church, VA
Edward Potter Sr.	(1836–1907)	private	A 115th Infantry		Rahway Cemetery	
Henry L. Potter	(d. 03.29.1907)	sergeant		12.01.64		
		promoted second lieutenant	114th Infantry	08.11.65	Rahway Cemetery	
John H. Potter	(d. 11.14.64)	private	G 4th Infantry	09.01.63–11.14.64	Presbyterian Cemetery, Westfield	died of disease
William E. Potter	(1840–1896)	captain	E 20th Infantry	02.09.64–08.07.65	Linden; Old Broad Street Presbyterian Church, Bridgeton, NJ	
William H. Powell	(b. 1845)	private	C 4th Infantry	09.01.63–01.19.65	Rahway	

Name	Birth–Death	Rank	Company	In–Out	Hometown or Burial Site	Miscellaneous
John S. Powers	(1842–10.09.62)	sergeant	G 31st Infantry		Plainfield	died of disease at Hilton Head, SC
William H. Powers	(1828–1879)	corporal	G 102nd Infantry	02.17.64–03.03.64		
		commissioned first lieutenant	G 25th Infantry	03.03.64–12.06.65	Baptist/Methodist Evergreen Cemetery, Plainfield	
Joseph H. Price	(d. 11.18.64)	private	D 32nd Infantry	02.23.64–11.18.64	Rahway Cemetery	died at Dutch Gap, VA; $300 UC bounty
Stephen Provost	(1830–06.07.65)	private	G 20th Infantry	01.65–06.07.65	Plainfield	died at Corps d' Afrique Hospital, New Orleans
Isaiah Queman	(d. 11.02.1916)	corporal	D 41st Infantry	09.30.64–11.10.65	Baptist/Methodist Evergreen Cemetery, Plainfield	
Anthony Randolph	(1841–04.15.1906)	private	K 22nd Infantry	01.04.64–05.13.65	Rahway Cemetery	wounded at Petersburg, VA, on 08.18.64
Charles B. Randolph	(1844–06.02.1918)	captain	C 118th Infantry	10.19.64		
		private	A 7th Infantry	11.12.63–11.16.66	Hillside Cemetery, Scotch Plains	$100 UC bounty
Evan C. Randolph	(1833–09.08.97)	private	H 22nd Infantry	01.10.64–10.16.65	Rahway Cemetery	
George Randolph	(1814–01.10.84)	private	I 32nd Infantry	03.02.64–08.22.65	Baptist/Methodist Evergreen Cemetery, Plainfield	
George W. Randolph	(1845–04.05.1916)	private	I 32nd Infantry	03.02.64–08.22.65	Plainfield; Hillside Cemetery, Scotch Plains	
Henry C. Randolph	(b. 1839)	private	E 67th Infantry	02.02.65–07.26.65	Plainfield	credit to Rhode Island
James F. Randolph	(1839–04.11.1907)	private	I 132nd Infantry		Evergreen Cemetery, Scotch Plains	discharged for disability at Camp Farnum, MD

Name	Birth–Death	Rank	Company	In–Out	Hometown or Burial Site	Miscellaneous
Joseph C. Randolph	(b. 1843)	private	E 77th Infantry			
			E 20th Infantry		Plainfield	$100 UC bounty
Watson Randolph	(1831–03.30.1902)	private	Battery B 5th Heavy Artillery	01.07.65–12.01.65	Hillside Cemetery, Scotch Plains	credit to Massachusetts
William H. Randolph	(1831–03.08.1909)	private	B 20th Infantry	02.22.64–10.12.64	Rahway Cemetery	
William J. Randolph	(b. 1815)	private	B 20th Infantry	02.09.64–03.06.64	Rahway	discharged for disability
John H. Ray	(1840–12.21.74)	private	A 22nd Infantry	12.09.63		
		teamster	C 32nd Infantry	04.15.64–09.19.65	Evergreen Cemetery, Hillside	wounded 02.10.65 at James Island, SC; $300 UC bounty
Thomas Ray	(1842–06.27.1902)	private	L 11th Heavy Artillery	05.64–04.65		
		corporal	D 113th Infantry	04.01.65–04.09.66	Evergreen Cemetery, Hillside	
David Reed	(1845–12.12.65)	private	I 31st Infantry	08.25.64–02.12.65		
			A 22nd Infantry	12.07.63–10.16.65	Elizabeth; Alexandria National Cemetery, VA	
James H. Reeves		private	E 16th Infantry			
			C 61st Infantry	02.01.64–04.30.66	Elizabeth	
James Riley	(1843–11.10.64)	private	B 25th Infantry	01.15.64–11.10.64	Salisbury National Cemetery, Salisbury, NC	died while a prisoner of war in Salisbury Prison, Salisbury
Nathan S. Roberts	(d. 07.24.1926)	assistant surgeon	21st Infantry		Fairview Cemetery, Westfield	

Name	Birth–Death	Rank	Company	In–Out	Hometown or Burial Site	Miscellaneous
Samuel L. Roberts	(1822–1881)	private	C 10th Infantry	11.20.63–02.26.64	Mt. Laurel Cemetery, Burlington County	$300 UC bounty
Cornelius Robinson	(d. 06.03.1916)	private	I 22nd Infantry	01.05.64–10.01.65	Evergreen Cemetery, Hillside	
John B. Robinson	(d. 08.20.1919)	private	I 20th Infantry	10.06.64–10.07.65	Rahway Cemetery	
John Howard Robinson	(1842–10.22.64)	private	B 43rd Infantry	03.16.64–04.07.64	Linden; Cypress Hill Cemetery, Brooklyn, NY	died at Camp William Penn, Philadelphia, PA
Joseph C. Robinson	(1840–10.29.78)	private	H 127 Infantry	09.01.64–09.07.65	Rahway Cemetery	
Peter Robinson	(1844–04.02.1910)	private	H 127th Infantry	09.01.64–09.07.65		
		corporal	E 54th Massachusetts Infantry	03.30.63		
		reduced to private			Rosehill Cemetery, Linden.	
Samuel L. Robinson	(1843–02.25.83)	private	A 41st Infantry	09.03.64–09.30.65	Rahway Cemetery	
Thomas Peter Robinson	(1844–05.20.1906)	private	A 54st Massachusetts Infantry	05.07.63	Section F, Soldiers Plot, Hazelwood Cemetery, Rahway	wounded 07.18.63 at Fort Wagner, SC
Elihu H. Ropes	(1845–1898)	second lieutenant, acting adjutant	23rd Infantry		Elizabeth; Baptist/Methodist Evergreen Cemetery, Plainfield	resigned due to reduction in army rank
George H. Ropes		captain	19th Infantry	12.08.63–08.22.65	Plainfield	
James Ross	(d. 11.23.1921)	captain	E 59th Infantry			
			D 11th Heavy Artillery	01.01.64	Fairview Cemetery, Westfield	

Name	Birth–Death	Rank	Company	In–Out	Hometown or Burial Site	Miscellaneous
John D. Ross	(1840–10.08.64)	private	C 4th Infantry	09.01.63–10.08.64	Springfield Presbyterian Cemetery	wounded at Petersburg, VA, 06.15.64; died of wounds
Joseph Ross	(d. 10.16.1900)	private	E 25th Infantry	01.19.64–12.06.65	Colored Map 4 Division, Row 4 Adult, Grave A; Evergreen Cemetery, Hillside	
William H. Ross	(d. 04.02.65)	private	H 24th Infantry	03.09.65–04.02.65	Union	died at Camp William Penn, Cheltenham, PA
Archer V. Rossell	(d. 1865)	sergeant	B 54th Infantry	1864–1865	Rahway; National Cemetery, Little Rock, AR	
John Ryan	(d. 10.03.65)	commissioned second lieutenant	E 118th Infantry		Linden; Gettysburg Cemetery, PA	died of wounds at Brownsville, TX
Elcazer Ryno	(d. 12.05.98)	private	I 2nd Infantry	02.63–01.64	Rahway Cemetery	
George R. Saddler	(1841–05.23.93)	corporal	C 32nd Infantry	02.20.64–08.22.65		
		reduced to private		01.01.65	Hillside Cemetery, Scotch Plains	
James Sales	(b. 1838)	private	18th Infantry			discharged for disability; $300 bounty 1st Ward, Elizabeth
Jonathan B. Sanders	(b. 1839)	corporal	F 50th Infantry	03.11.65–07.30.65	Rahway	
George A. Sayers	(d. 02.24.1909)	private	Battery D U.S. Colored Heavy Artillery	01.01.64–10.02.65	Evergreen Cemetery, Hillside	

Name	Birth–Death	Rank	Company	In–Out	Hometown or Burial Site	Miscellaneous
Peter Schenk		musician	G 41st Infantry	10.05.64–10.27.64	Plainfield	
William A. Scott	(1833–07.04.64)	sergeant	G 20th Infantry	02.09.64–03.06.64		
		private	D 8th Infantry	10.63–07.04.64	West Indies; Elizabeth; Grave 2864 Andersonville National Cemetery, Andersonville, GA	died of disease as a prisoner of war at Andersonville, GA
Thomas B. Scudder	(1827–06.12.82)	private	F 25th Infantry	03.04.65–12.06.65	Rahway Cemetery	
Samuel Sharp	(b. 1842)	private	C 4th Infantry	09.01.63–06.16.65	Linden	discharged 09.29.64 for wound in forearm at Chaffin's Farm, VA; hospitalized at Balfour Hospital, Hampton, VA
George W. Shields	(d. 10.12.93)	private	9th Infantry			
		corporal	1st Regiment, Kansas Colored Infantry		Elizabeth; Johnson Cemetery, Camden, Camden County	discharged 07.12.65
John H. Simmons	(1840–08.10.64)	private	D 30th Infantry	03.18.64–08.10.64	buried on 07.16.1906, Section E–Green, Evergreen Cemetery, Hillside	wounded 07.30.64 at Petersburg, VA; died of wounds
William H. Simms	(1841–11.05.1909)	private	A 127th Infantry			
		private	H 38th Infantry		Elizabeth; buried Mount Hope United Methodist Church Cemetery, Salem, Salem County	prisoner of war 12.15.64, Murfreesboro, TN
Samuel Slater		first sergeant	A 1st Cavalry	1863–11.18.65	Linden	$100 UC bounty

Name	Birth–Death	Rank	Company	In–Out	Hometown or Burial Site	Miscellaneous
John Sloan		musician	2nd Infantry Brigade Band			
		sergeant	B 108th Infantry	06.29.64–01.65	Elizabeth; New Somerville Cemetery, Somerville, Somerset County	
Charles Smalley	(1844–08.14.71)	private	F 37th Infantry		Plot 47, Evergreen Cemetery, Hillside	
George F. Smith	(1832–05.31.1916)	private	C 20th Infantry			
		private	L 2nd Cavalry		England; Evergreen Cemetery, Hillside	
George Washington Smith	(1842–12.24.99)	sergeant	I 20th Infantry	08.29.64–08.29.65	Elizabeth; Evergreen Cemetery, Hillside	
John H. Smith	(1846–1879)	private	H 4th Infantry	09.01.63–06.26.65	Elizabeth	
John W.B. Smith	(1821–11.14.63)	private	A 20th Infantry			
			B 26th Infantry			
			E 19th Infantry Springfield			died at USA Hospital, Portsmouth Grove, RI; $300 UC bounty
Thomas F. Smith	(1845–1888)	private	A 31st Infantry	08.03.64–11.07.65	Rahway	$300 bounty 3rd Ward, Elizabeth
Walter G. Smith	(1842–1869)	private	K 43rd Infantry			
			B 62nd Infantry		Hillside Cemetery, Scotch Plains	
Charles Stansbury	(1840–02.19.94)	private	I 25th Infantry	03.01.65–12.06.65	Rahway Cemetery	
Francis Stansbury	(d. 04.08.94)	private	E 20th Infantry		Baptist/Evergreen Methodist Cemetery, Plainfield	

Name	Birth–Death	Rank	Company	In–Out	Hometown or Burial Site	Miscellaneous
Benjamin W. Stevenson	(d. 09.17.92)	private	H 3rd Infantry			
		private	A 43rd Infantry		Elizabeth; Evergreen Cemetery, Hillside	
John E. Stewart	(1842–10.10.1925)	first lieutenant	D 9th Infantry	11.30.63–12.17.64		
		promoted adjutant to field and staff	Company C	12.28.63	Linden; Hillside Cemetery, Scotch Plains	
William S. Stewart	(1842–1900)	assistant surgeon	83rd Infantry	08.17.63–07.20.64	Ireland; Baptist/Methodist Evergreen Cemetery, Plainfield	trained at Free Military School for Applicants for Commands of Colored Troops
Charles R. Still	(1834–07.29.1905)	private	C 20th Infantry	02.09.64–08.05.64		
			H 45th Infantry	08.06.64–11.04.65	Elizabethtown; Evergreen Cemetery, Hillside	
William Still		private	G 37th Infantry	06.13.64–10.01.64	Linden	
George A. Sutphen	(1838–11.23.1909)	private	B 22nd Infantry	01.09.64–10.16.65	Martinique; Hillside Cemetery, Scotch Plains	
James Sutphen	(b. 1843)	private	B 41st Infantry	09.20.64–12.10.65	Westfield	
Benjamin Sutton	(1837–1907)	corporal	H 80th Infantry		Hillside Cemetery, Scotch Plains	
Alpheus Taylor	(1838–03.29.83)	private	K 22nd Infantry	01.04.64–10.16.65	Westfield; Rahway Cemetery	
George W. Taylor		private	A 22nd Infantry	09.30.64–10.16.65		Medal of Honor
William H. Thomas	(1837–01.13.98)	private	A 127th Infantry	05.14.64–10.20.65	Linden; Rahway Cemetery, Hillside	
Amos Thompson	(1832–1880)	corporal	A 127th Infantry	09.01.64–09.07.65	Rahway	
Charles H. Thompson	(1843–08.05.93)	private	D 20th Infantry	02.09.64–10.07.65	Evergreen Cemetery, Hillside	

Name	Birth–Death	Rank	Company	In–Out	Hometown or Burial Site	Miscellaneous
Charles K.I. Thompson	(d. 03.20.81)	private	F 25th Infantry	02.20.65–12.06.65	Rahway Cemetery	
Edward G. Thompson	(1820–01.20.1906)	private	A 22nd Infantry	12.29.64–10.16.65		
			B 43rd Infantry	03.16.64–04.05.64	Elizabeth; Evergreen Cemetery, Hillside	
Jacob Thompson	(1846–1910)	private	E 20th Infantry	04.29.64–10.07.65	Elizabeth	
Thomas H. Thompson		private	D 41st Infantry	09.20.64–09.30.65	Hazelwood Cemetery, Rahway	
George Thornton		private	F 2nd Cavalry	09.06.64–05.15.65	Linden	
Samuel M. Till	(1835–1904)	private	C 54th Massachusetts Infantry	12.11.63–08.20.65	Baptist/Methodist Evergreen Cemetery, Plainfield	
Leander Tines		private	F 22nd Infantry	12.29.64–10.16.65		$100 Elizabeth bounty
Aaron S. Truhardt		private	H 127th Infantry	09.01.64–09.07.65	Elizabeth; Moore's Farm Cemetery, Stoutsburg, Mercer County	
Charles Tunison	(b. 1842)	private	D 23rd Infantry	06.16.64–11.30.65	Elizabethtown	credit to Massachusetts
Daniel Tunison	(d. 02.17.77)				Evergreen Cemetery, Hillside	
Francis Tunison	(1823-01.10.89)	private	B 20th Infantry	02.09.64–10.17.65	Rahway Cemetery	
John Oliver Tunison Jr.	(1823–1883)	private	A 2nd Cavalry	09.07.64–06.29.65	Summit	
William B. Tunison		private	A 2nd Cavalry	08.31.64–06.29.65	Evergreen Cemetery, Hillside	
John B. Turner	(1844–1882)	private	I 2nd Infantry	02.29.64–09.12.65	Rahway Cemetery	
Samuel Turner	(b. 1843)	private	A 27th Infantry	01.16.64–09.21.65	Cranford	

Name	Birth–Death	Rank	Company	In–Out	Hometown or Burial Site	Miscellaneous
William H. Turner	(1838–05.27.64)	private	K 22nd Infantry	01.04.64–05.06.64	Hazelwood Cemetery, Rahway	wounded at Wilderness, VA; died after amputation of leg
George Tuttle	(b. 1836)	private	K 68th Infantry	03.11.64	Elizabeth	
William H. Vanderveer	(1843–01.1922)	private	H 127th Infantry	08.30.64–09.07.65	Plainfield; Elmwood Cemetery, New Brunswick, Middlesex County	
Henry S. Vandeveer	(1843–03.03.1932)	musician	C 127th Infantry			
		private	A 127th Infantry	08.24.64–09.08.65	Cranford; Fairview Cemetery, Westfield	
Philip M. van Hise	(d. 02.15.65)	private	F 41st Infantry	09.23.64–02.15.65	Plainfield; National Cemetery, City Point, VA	died at U.S. Army General Hospital, Points of Rocks, VA
William van Horn	(d. 08.30.87)	private	H 43rd Infantry	05.09.64–10.20.65	Plainfield; Lamington Colored Cemetery, Lamington, Somerset County	
James C. van Houten	(b. 1842)	private	A 22nd Infantry			
		corporal		06.29.65		$100 UC bounty
James/Jacob D. van Pelt	(d. 07.9.63)	private	F 41st Infantry	09.24.64–09.30.65	Elizabeth; Gettysburg National Cemetery; removed and buried 03.08.1899 at Van Liew Cemetery, North Brunswick, Middlesex County	died of wounds at Gettysburg
John van Riper	(b. 1845)	corporal	M 2nd Cavalry	09.02.63–11.01.65		
		promoted corporal		07.12.65	Linden	
Albert van Sickles	(1822–1880)	private	I 51st Infantry		Linden	$100 UC bounty

Name	Birth–Death	Rank	Company	In–Out	Hometown or Burial Site	Miscellaneous
Theodore Vreeland		private	1st Cavalry	12.28.63		
			K 43rd Infantry	02.25.65–10.20.65	Linden	
John Wallace	(b. 1837)	private	D 32nd Infantry	02.23.64–08.22.65	Linden	
Charles W. Ward	(b. 1838)	private	E 43rd Infantry	03.31.64–10.20.65	Rahway	
William J. Ward	(1843–1884)	corporal	I 19th Infantry	01.16.64–01.15.67	Hazelwood Cemetery, Rahway	wounded at Walthall, VA
John Warfield	(d. 01.08.64)	corporal	G 4th Infantry	09.01.63–01.08.64	Rahway	killed in action
George F. Watson	(b. 1836)	commissioned first lieutenant	2nd Louisiana Native Guard			resigned 05.30.63 for reasons of prejudice
			I 31st Infantry	08.25.64–12.09.65	Elizabeth	
Thomas F. Watson	(1844–09.22.64)	private	K 31st Infantry	12.20.64	Linden; Andersonville Cemetery, GA	
Charles H. Weeks	(b. 1837)	corporal	H 22nd Infantry	01.01.64–03.23.65	Elizabeth	discharged 09.30.64 for severe wound in right arm (amputated) received at Fort Harrison, VA
Nathaniel Weeks	(1845–11.26.64)	sergeant	I 43rd Infantry	05.23.64–11.25.64	Elizabeth; Cypress Hill Cemetery, Long Island, NY	
Charles White	(b. 1841)	private	I 31st Infantry	08.25.64–12.09.65	Linden	substitute for H.S. Hubbell
George A. White	(1839–03.03.95)	private	F 25th Infantry	03.04.65–12.06.65	Rahway Cemetery	
James H. White	(1840–12.27.1929)	private	A 41st Infantry	11.28.64–10.10.65	Fairview Cemetery, Westfield	
Louis F. White	(1844–1903)	private	H 14th Heavy Artillery	10.09.64–06.30.65	Rahway Cemetery	

Name	Birth–Death	Rank	Company	In–Out	Hometown or Burial Site	Miscellaneous
George W. Whitehead		private	B 36th Infantry	04.64–05.65	Elizabeth; Evergreen Cemetery, Hillside	
George W. Whitney	(1834–04.29.65)	corporal	D 20th Infantry	02.09.64–04.29.65	Elizabeth	
Henry A. Whitney	(1844–12.30.1924)	captain	K 33rd Infantry	01.31.63–01.31.66		
		commissioned second lieutenant	B 45th Infantry			
		first lieutenant	H 45th Infantry	08.20.65	Division 1, Section D, Plot 88, Row 20, Hillside Cemetery, Scotch Plains	served April–May recruiting black soldiers in West Virginia; trained at Free Military School for Applicants for Commands of Colored Troops, Philadelphia
Charles A. Williams	(b. 1842)	private	H 127th Infantry	09.01.64–10.20.65	Elizabeth	
Frederick L. Williams		private	K 38th Infantry	09.06.64–06.30.65	Linden	
Isaiah Williams		private	G 43rd Infantry	04.16.64–06.22.65	Presbyterian Cemetery, Springfield	
James H. Williams	(1831–04.08.94)	private	F 20th Infantry	02.09.64–09.30.64	Elizabeth; Evergreen Cemetery, Hillside	
John C. Williams Jr.	(1837–1865)	private	A 41st Infantry	09.02.64–09.30.65		
			H 25th Infantry	02.16.65–12.06.65	Evergreen Cemetery, Hillside	$300 UC bounty
Robert S. Williams	(d. 07.13.1918)	private	A 41st Infantry		Evergreen Cemetery, Hillside	wounded 05.16.64 at Drury's Bluff, VA

Name	Birth–Death	Rank	Company	In–Out	Hometown or Burial Site	Miscellaneous
William H. Williams	(1836–1911)	private	I 20th Infantry	02.09.64 10.07.65		
		promoted corporal		02.09.64		
		reduced to private		02.13.64	England; Baptist/Methodist Evergreen Cemetery, Plainfield	captured 05.16.64 at Drury's Bluff, VA
Lewis Williamson	(d. 09.12.86)		B 4th Heavy Artillery			
			B 113th Infantry		Evergreen Cemetery, Hillside	
Charles H. Wilson	(b. 1843)	private	H 43rd Infantry	04.28.64–10.20.65	Elizabethtown	wounded 05.14.64 in right thigh at Drury's Bluff
James Wilson	(1828–1895)	sergeant	F 20th Infantry	02.09.64–10.07.65	Evergreen Cemetery, Hillside	slave prior to 04.19.61
Washington O. Wilson	(1846–1881)	sergeant	D 18th Infantry	08.64–09.65		
			D 101st Infantry		Linden; Rahway Cemetery	
Amos T. Wood	(1843–03.13.81)	private	H 127 Infantry	08.31.64–10.20.65	Rahway Cemetery	$300 Rahway bounty
Cuff Wood	(1831–1868)	private	H 127th Infantry	08.31.64–10.20.65	Fairview Cemetery, Westfield	
Henry Wood	(1839–05.26.1909)	private	C 29th Connecticut Infantry			
		sergeant	I 20th Infantry	02.9.64–10.07.65	Rosehill Cemetery, Linden	
William B. Wright	(1840–08.21.84)	commissioned captain	C 25th Infantry	01.26.64–12.06.65	Section M, Grave 783, Rahway Cemetery	trained at Free Military School for Commands of Colored Troops, Philadelphia, PA

Name	Birth–Death	Rank	Company	In–Out	Hometown or Burial Site	Miscellaneous
Benjamin Wyckoff		private	B 25th Infantry	01.07.64–12.06.65		
			K 43rd Infantry	03.16.65–10.20.65	Baptist/Methodist Evergreen Cemetery, Plainfield	
Charles Wyckoff	(d. 08.26.76)	private	D 26th Infantry	02.27.64–08.28.65	Rahway Cemetery	
Hiram G. Wyckoff	(b. 1839)	private	A 3rd Heavy Artillery	06.05.63–04.26.64	Plainfield	intraregimental transfers from Company A to B; Company B to H
Thomas Wyckoff	(b. 1844)	first sergeant	D 25th Infantry	01.19.64–09.19.65		
		promoted second lieutenant		11.28.65	Plainfield	
William S.H. Young		private	H 3rd Infantry	07.18.63–10.31.65	Rahway	
Nicholas Zabriskie		private	I 45th Infantry	07.30.64–11.04.65	Elizabeth	

Appendix C

United States Navy and Marine Corps

Enlistments in the United States Navy and Marine Corps were made at naval depots. Recruits were allowed to select the place of credit, and the provost marshal of the district was notified. Enlistments for the naval service were for one, two and three years and, for the Marine Corps, four years. Free men of African descent were described as mulatto, Negro, black or yellow.

Sailors	B/D	Rank	Vessel(s)	Dates of service	Country of birth	Race	Hometown/ burial site	State credit	Navy Medal
Robert A. Aaron	(1822–04.12.63)	landsman	USS *Crusader*	09.19.62–07.31.63		Negro	Rahway		
George W. Ackerman	(1845–1884)	seaman	USS *Winona*	11.11.61–01.07.65			Elizabeth		
William H. Ackerman	(1841–07.02.63)	landsman	USS *Valley City*			Negro	Elizabeth		
Thomas B. Anderson	(1845–1886)	first class boy	USS *Carrabasset*	06.29.61–02.07.62					
		seaman	USS *Vandalia*	08.16.64–06.26.65		Negro		NY	
James H. Avery	(1825–10.11.98)	seaman	USS *Metacomet*	08.11.62–06.06.65	Scotland		Rahway Cemetery		✓
Henry Baker	(1828–1882)	seaman	USS *North Carolina*	06.03.64–07.21.66			Elizabeth		
Charles H. Baldwin	(1839–11.22.1911)	coal heaver/ ordinary seaman	USS *Wyalusing*						
			USS *Ohio*						
			USS *Connecticut*						
			USS *Savannah*	11.03.63–11.29.64			Rahway; buried at Christ Church Cemetery, Accokeek, Maryland	MA	
William H. Baldwin	(1840–1881)	coal heaver	USS *Princeton*	02.28.64–03.28.65			Rahway Cemetery		
George W. Bennett	(1843–06.15.63)	seaman	USS *Saratoga*	07.09.62–06.15.63			Elizabeth; Hazelwood Cemetery, Rahway		

Sailors	B/D	Rank	Vessel(s)	Dates of service	Country of birth	Race	Hometown/ burial site	State credit	Navy Medal
John H. Bennett	(1838–1892)	landsman	USS *Savanna*						
			USS *Charles Phelps*	09.18.61–07.12.65		black	Evergreen Cemetery, Elizabeth		
Charles J.B. Benson	(1839–1881)	ordinary seaman	USS *Ohio*	08.26.61–08.21.63					
		landsman	USS *Harcourt*	08.18.64–03.31.65		black	Plainfield	MA	
William Braden	(d. 01.17.90)						Evergreen Cemetery, Elizabeth		
Peter Brandt		seaman	USS *Princeton*	01.14.65–12.17.65			Elizabeth		
Michael Breen	(1846–1912)	second class boy	USS *Ohio*	04.10.61–08.7.61					
		landsman	USS *Ohio*	07.19.64			Fairview Cemetery, Westfield	MA	
Jacob Brinkerhoff	(d. 1885)	landsman				Negro	Fairview Cemetery, Westfield	NY	
James H. Brown	(1843–1885)	landsman	USS *Horace Beals*	05.20.64–12.31.64					
		quartermaster	USS *Albatross*			Negro	Rahway		✓
Theodore Brown	(b. 1841)	landsman	USS *Keystone State*	04.01.63–09.08.63		Negro		NY	
Titus C. Brown	(1842–11.22.84)	seaman	USS *Nantucket*	05.06.63–07.01.64		Negro	Rahway		

Sailors	B/D	Rank	Vessel(s)	Dates of service	Country of birth	Race	Hometown/ burial site	State credit	Navy Medal
John Burke	(1840–03.24.93)	coal heaver	USS *Ohio*						
			USS Mercedita	11.29.61–06.18.63			soldiers plot, Fairview Cemetery, Westfield	MA	
John Burns	(1842–04.15.97)	seaman	USS *Lackawanna*						
		ordinary seaman	USS *Lenapee*	10.11.64–10.03.67			Rahway		
Robert J. Carroll	(1844–01.21.1917)	first class boy	USS *Muscoota*	09.20.64–03.10.66					
		landsman	USS *Ohio*	01.08.64–01.30.65				MA	
John Cary	(1838–06.27.94)	landsman	USS *Constitution*	09.26.61–04.15.62					
		ordinary seaman	USS *North Carolina*	11.26.64–10.28.67			Evergreen Cemetery, Elizabeth		
John Case	(b. 1843)	first class boy	USS *Benton*			black			
William G. Casner	(1843–08.28.1916)	steering steward	USS *Lenapee*	01.25.65–01.27.67					
William H. Chew		coal heaver	USS *North Carolina*	09.01.64–06.06.65					
Amos Clark	(1808–1879)	coal heaver	USS *Ottawa*	09.06.64–08.12.65					
Oliver G.H. Clark	(d. 04.15.1911)	seaman					Mount Olivet Cemetery, Elizabeth		
Robert Clark	(1844–09.29.62)	landsman	USS *Wabash*	05.09.61–04.01.63		mulatto	Westfield		

Sailors	B/D	Rank	Vessel(s)	Dates of service	Country of birth	Race	Hometown/ burial site	State credit	Navy Medal
Charles J. Clifford	(d. 03.02.1910)	ordinary seaman		11.23.61–09.30.63			Elizabeth Evergreen Cemetery, Hillside		
William Cochrane	(1843–06.16.64)	fireman	USS sloop *Savannah*	08.30.61–09.28.64			buried at Presbyterian Cemetery, New Providence		
Patrick Connelly	(b. 1838)	landsman	USS *Princeton*						
			USS *Hartford*	11.26.61–12.15.63	Dublin, Ireland	black			
Samuel Conover	(1842–1891)	landsman	assigned to Navy Yard at Norfolk, VA	11.17.63–11.16.64		mulatto			
William Conover	(1840–1878)	coal heaver	USS *Princeton*	09.5.64–10.02.65					
John L. Conway	(b. 1849)	ordinary seaman	USS *Maumee*	09.08.64–11.17.64					
		fireman	USS *Boston*	02.01.65–01.13.68		Negro			
Charles Cook	(b. 1843)	landsman	USS *Clematis/ Tonawanda*	09.14.64–10.01.66		Negro	Elizabethtown		
William H. Cook	(1845–04.05.1914)	landsman	USS *Vicksburg*	10.17.62–12.31.64		Negro	Elizabeth; buried in Section E-Green, Evergreen Cemetery, Hillside		
John T. Cox	(b. 1849)	landsman	USS *Winooski*	05.08.64–04.11.66		Negro		NY	
Jeremiah A. Cromwell	(1830–1875)	landsman					Rahway; buried at Rahway Cemetery		

Sailors	B/D	Rank	Vessel(s)	Dates of service	Country of birth	Race	Hometown/ burial site	State credit	Navy Medal
Oliver Cromwell	(b. 1843)	landsman	USS *Princeton*	11.03.63–10.27.64		Negro	Elizabethtown		
Jeremiah Crowley	(1842–06.09.81)	landsman	USS *Corina*	12.05.61–12.04.67					
			USS *Princeton*	04.22.64–05.08.65			Elizabeth	MA	
Walton Darby	(d. 09.06.1920)	midshipman	United States Naval Reading Class				Elizabeth		
George Davis	(1841–02.03.94)	landsman	USS *Memphis*	09.03.63–10.01.64		Negro	Elizabeth; Evergreen Cemetery, Hillside		
William H. Day	(1847–09.08.1926)	landsman	USS *Princeton*	08.12.64–09.30.65					
William H. DeCamp	(d. 07.04.98)	fireman first class	USS *Rhode Island*	07.16.61–01.18.62			Elizabeth		
William H. DeHart	(1838–1863)	landsman		05.30.63			Elizabeth		
James G. Denton							Evergreen Cemetery, Hillside		
George W. Disbrow		landsman	USS *Montgomery*	08.11.64–06.20.65			Elizabeth		
Sylvester Doremus	(1831–1907)	landsman	USS *Agawan*	07.23.64–06.30.65	England	Negro	Rahway	NY	
Matthew Dowd	(1846–09.26.86)	landsman	USS *North Carolina*						
			USS *Lenapee*	07.25.64–07.27.67			Evergreen Cemetery, Hillside		

Sailors	B/D	Rank	Vessel(s)	Dates of service	Country of birth	Race	Hometown/ burial site	State credit	Navy Medal
George W. Drake	(1842–06.07.65)	hospital steward	USS *Steamer*	08.10.63–06.07.65			Linden; Evergreen Cemetery, Hillside		
Willis Sanford Drake	(1843–02.07.1926)	second class gunner	USS *Monitor*						
			USS frigate *Potomac*				buried at Evergreen Cemetery, Hillside		
Edward Du Bois	(b. 1836)	landsman	USS *Potomac*	08.02.64–03.31.66	Nassau, New Providence		Elizabeth		
David H. Dunham	(b. 1842)	seaman	USS *Ohio*						
			USS *Tuscarora*	06.13.64–06.13.64				MA	
Samuel H. Dunham	(1841–1902)	landsman	USS *Wamsutta*	03.15.62–12.31.64		mulatto	Plainfield		
William H. Dunn	(1848–06.30.1900)	seaman	USS *Morse*	07.01.61–06.19.62					
		acting masters mate	USS *Monadnock*	1864–1865			Elizabeth		✓
William A. Edgerton	(1833–1888)	landsman	USS *Princeton*	08.19.64–06.27.65			Elizabeth; Evergreen Cemetery, Elizabeth		
Thomas Ellis	(b. 1841)	landsman	U.S. Navy Marine Corps	10.10.64–06.25.65			Rahway		
William Ellis		coal heaver	USS *Massachusetts*	08.31.63–08.30.64					
		fireman	USS *Massachusetts*						
			USS *Estrella*	10.26.64–10.24.66					

Sailors	B/D	Rank	Vessel(s)	Dates of service	Country of birth	Race	Hometown/ burial site	State credit	Navy Medal
Charles M. Fay	(1842–1868)	landsman	USS *Ohio*						
			USS *Princeton*	07.21.62–07.19.64			Evergreen Cemetery, Hillside		
Benjamin Ferguson	(1840–1864)	landsman	USS *Stettinn*	08.25.63–09.30.64		Negro	Rahway		
James W. Fisher	(1843–1884)	landsman	USS *Tioga*	07.15.64–03.31.66	British Honduras/ Belize	Negro	Evergreen Cemetery, Elizabeth		
John P. Fox							Mt. Olivet Cemetery, Elizabeth		
William E. Gale	(b. 1845)	third class boy	USS *Richmond*	01.01.63–06.30.65		Negro	Plainfield		
James K. Giles	(b. 1842)	landsman				mulatto	Elizabeth		
William J. Gould	(b. 1843)	landsman	USS *Maumee*	08.23.64–03.31.65	Jamaica		Rahway		
Robert Graham	(1837–1916)	landsman	USS *Tacony*	10.64–07.65			Evergreen Cemetery, Hillside		✓
James Hall	(1840–09.20.84)	landsman	USS *North Carolina*	08.26.63–07.31.64			Elizabeth		
Henry W. Hand	(1841–1905)	acting quartermaster	USS *New Hampshire*	11.13.61–02.21.66					
		acting master	U.S. storeship *Vermont*	1863–1864					
John H. Harrison	(b. 1826)	landsman	USS *Mohican*	10.07.61–12.14.64					
		Fireman	USS *Glaucus*	12.14.64–06.05.65		mulatto	Port Elizabeth		

Sailors	B/D	Rank	Vessel(s)	Dates of service	Country of birth	Race	Hometown/ burial site	State credit	Navy Medal
Charles Hawkins	(1834–1924)	seaman	USS *Agawam*	04.25.64–06.22.67	Canada		Evergreen Cemetery, Hillside		✓
Isaiah Hedden	(b. 1838)	landsman	USS *Water Witch*	09.01.63		Negro	Rahway		
Lydack Hedden	(b. 1842)	landsman	USS *Governor Buckingham*	10.27.63–12.31.64		mulatto	Rahway		
William Henry	(1842–04.26.1906)	officer's cook	USS *Dawn*	05.11.62–03.31.63					
		landsman	USS *Lady Sterling*						
			USS *Hornet*	08.29.64–11.22.66	British North America	Negro	Evergreen Cemetery, Hillside	NY	
Thomas Higgins	(1824–11.18.95)	landsman	USS *North Carolina*	05.27.61–05.30.62			Mt. Olivet Cemetery, Elizabeth		
William E. Hill	(1838–02.01.1913)	seaman	USS *North Carolina*	09.23.62–10.07.63			Evergreen Cemetery, Hillside		
George L. Holland	(1842–1909)	first class boy	USS *Grand Gulf*	08.03.63					
		seaman	USS *Lackawanna*	05.28.64–07.01.65	Sandwich Islands	Negro	buried at Fairview Cemetery, Westfield	NY	
John Holland	(b. 1837)	ordinary seaman	USS *Minnesota*	12.23.62–12.31.63	St. Thomas	Negro	Westfield		
Jacob P.J. Howard	(b. 1838)	landsman	USS *Wanderer*	05.11.64–06.30.65		Negro	Rahway	NY	
William H. Hughes	(1819–09.21.1909)	boy	USS *Ohio*	08.18.64–08.17.65			Rahway Cemetery		

Sailors	B/D	Rank	Vessel(s)	Dates of service	Country of birth	Race	Hometown/ burial site	State credit	Navy Medal
Henry Hull		landsman	USS *Glaucus*	08.10.64–06.05.65					
Thomas R. Hunt		landsman	USS *Princeton*	09.05.64–09.30.65			Rahway		
William H. Jackson	(b. 1835)	seaman				mulatto	Elizabeth		
Adolphus J. Johnson Jr.	(d. 11.09.63)	first class boy	USS *Adela*	07.10.63–11.09.63			Elizabeth		
John H. Johnson	(b. 1840)	landsman	USS *Dacotah*						
			USS *Monadnock*	08.31.63–10.25.65		Negro	Rahway Cemetery		
William H. Johnson	(1842)	landsman	USS *Iosco*						
			USS *Savannah*	07.13.64		Negro			
Albert G. Jones	(1806–09.16.75)						Rahway Cemetery		
Henry M. Jones	(b. 1842)	landsman	USS *Wyandank*	08.30.64–07.01.65	Jamaica	Negro	Plot 77, Evergreen Cemetery, Hillside		
William H. Jones	(1843–12.20.90)	landsman	USS *Monticello*						
			USS *Ohio*						
		captain of the top	USS *Richmond*	08.05.64		mulatto	Plainfield		✓
Joseph H. King	(1845–07.13.64)	seaman	USS *Minnesota*						
			USS *Fahkee*						
			USS *Sangamon*	06.19.61–08.12.65	Lisbon, Portugal	mulatto	Rahway		

Sailors	B/D	Rank	Vessel(s)	Dates of service	Country of birth	Race	Hometown/ burial site	State credit	Navy Medal
William N. King	(1841–1926)	seaman	gunboat *Cincinnati*	02.21.62–11.14.62					
			U.S. Marine Corps	04.19.64–08.26.65			Elizabeth; Evergreen Cemetery, Hillside		
John Lee	(b. 1836)	landsman	USS *Princeton*	08.16.64–06.22.65			Elizabeth		
Peter Lee		landsman	USS *North Carolina*	12.12.64–06.18.65		colored	Elizabeth		
William H. Lee	(1841–01.31.1903)	seaman	USS *North Carolina*	09.05.62–06.05.65			Evergreen Cemetery, Elizabeth		
Henry H. Leeds	(d. 08.21.1915)						Elizabeth; Evergreen Cemetery, Elizabeth		
John W. Long	(1846–03.04.1911)	quartermaster					Elizabeth; Evergreen Cemetery, Elizabeth		
William H. Manning	(b. 1843)	landsman	USS *Emma*	10.26.63–12.31.64		Negro	Plainfield		
Charles G. Marsh	(1844–06.12.1921)	landsman	USS *Niagara*	07.16.64–08.01.65			Evergreen Cemetery, Hillside		
Philip Marsh	(b. 1843)	landsman	USS *William Badger*	09.08.63–12.31.63		Negro	Westfield		
John McDonald	(1840–1894)	boatswain's mate	USS *Baron De Kalb*				Rahway	MA	✓
George W. Moore	(1840–05.06.1919)	seaman	USS *Rhode Island*	12.7.63–10.16.65			Hazelwood Cemetery, Rahway		✓
Cornelius Moris	(b. 1842)	landsman	USS *St. Mary's*	01.25.64–01.01.65	Elizabethport	Negro			

Sailors	B/D	Rank	Vessel(s)	Dates of service	Country of birth	Race	Hometown/ burial site	State credit	Navy Medal
William Morris		second class boy	USS *Georgia*	10.26.63–06.09.65					
Albert Morse		landsman	USS *Maumee*	08.26.64–06.17.65					
		promoted first class fireman		11.01.64		colored	Linden		
Robert Morse	(d. 10.05.89)	seaman	USS *Princeton*	02.04.65–05.19.66		colored	Rahway Cemetery		
John F. Murray	(b. 1840)	landsman	USS *Wissahickon*	06.24.62–06.25.65		mulatto	Elizabeth		
George W. Myers	(1835–05.17.1902)	landsman	USS *Santiago de Cuba*						
			USS *Huntsville*	01.31.63–04.01.64		mulatto	Evergreen Cemetery, Hillside	NY	
James H. Oliver	(b. 1845)	ordinary seaman	USS *Princeton*	10.10.63–11.21.64			Rahway		
William H. Oliver		landsman	USS *Sabine*						
			USS *Niagara*			Negro	Rahway		
James Parker	(b. 1842)	ordinary seaman	USS *Union*						
		coal heaver	USS *Isonomia*	08.09.64–01.01.65	Norway	Negro	Rahway Cemetery		
William Pease	(1842–12.23.64)	first class boy	USS *Unadilla*			mulatto	Elizabeth		
Joseph H. Post	(1838–06.01.63)	landsman	USS *Congress*	10.03.61–03.18.62	Elizabethtown	mulatto			

Sailors	B/D	Rank	Vessel(s)	Dates of service	Country of birth	Race	Hometown/ burial site	State credit	Navy Medal
William E. Potter	(1840–1896)	seaman	USS *Ohio*	04.14.65–01.27.68			Linden		
William H. Powell	(1828–11.22.79)	seaman	USS *North Carolina*						
			USS *Potomac*	07.22.61–07.06.63			Baptist/Methodist Evergreen Cemetery, Plainfield		
Charles E. Randolph	(b. 1844)	landsman	USS *Richmond*	05.31.64–06.30.65		Negro	Plainfield		
George W. Randolph	(1845–1916)	landsman	USS *Richmond*	05.31.64–06.30.65		Negro	Plainfield		
James F. Randolph	(1839–04.11.1907)	landsman		06.07.61–05.28.64		Negro	Linden		
Samuel F. Randolph		seaman					grave B-25-A-8 at Hillside Cemetery		
John H. Ray	(1840–12.21.74)	landsman	USS *New Ironsides*	10.25.61–02.10.64		mulatto	Elizabeth; Evergreen Cemetery, Hillside		
David Reed	(1845–12.12.65)	landsman	USS *Wabash*						
			USS *Augusta Dinsmore*	07.26.62–03.31.64		mulatto		NY	
James Riley	(1843–11.10.64)	landsman	USS *Connecticut*	12.22.62–08.11.63					
		ordinary seaman	U.S. Marine Corps	04.28.64–09.14.64		mulatto	Elizabeth		
John Romain		second class boy	USS *Ohio*	04.20.61–08.01.63					

Sailors	B/D	Rank	Vessel(s)	Dates of service	Country of birth	Race	Hometown/ burial site	State credit	Navy Medal
Henry Rose	(b. 1823)	quartermaster	USS *North Carolina*	07.18.64–06.28.65	St. Johns, New Brunswick		Linden		
John Schenck		landsman	USS *Pontoosuc*	08.11.64–06.08.65			Rahway		
William H. Scott	(1837–1899)	acting gunner	USS *Cambridge*	08.03.63–07.24.65	West Indies	Negro	Elizabeth		
James Sickels	(b. 1832)	landsman			Canada	black	Elizabeth		
William H. Simms	(b. 1841)	seaman	USS *North Carolina*	05.21.64–04.01.65	Canada	Negro			
Charles Smalley	(1845–08.14.71)	first class boy	USS *Supply*	09.07.63–07.01.64		Negro	Plainfield; plot 47, Baptist/Methodist Evergreen Cemetery, Plainfield		
John W.B. Smith	(1821–11.04.63)	landsman	USS *Kennebec*	01.20.62		mulatto	Springfield		
Thomas F. Smith	(1845–1888)	seaman	USS *Hartford*	05.21.61–03.09.62					
			USS *Magnolia*	08.01.64–08.31.65		mulatto	Evergreen Cemetery, Hillside		✓
Henry C. Stanford	(b. 1843)	landsman	USS *South Carolina*				Evergreen Cemetery, Hillside		
George A. Sutphen	(1841–11.23.1909)	landsman	USS *Sabine*						
			USS *Camelia*	08.16.64–10.01.65	Martinique	Negro	Hillside Cemetery, Scotch Plains		
Charles H. Taylor	(b. 1840)	landsman	USS *Seneca*	09.03.64–06.08.65		mulatto	Rahway		

Sailors	B/D	Rank	Vessel(s)	Dates of service	Country of birth	Race	Hometown/ burial site	State credit	Navy Medal
John H. Thompson	(1846–1910)	landsman	USS *Huron*						
			USS *Princeton*	08.12.64–09.04.65		mulatto	Elizabeth		
Samuel M. Till	(1835–02.11.65)	landsman	USS *Restless*						
			USS *Pursuit*	05.16.63–12.30.64			Hillside Cemetery, Scotch Plains		
John B. Turner	(1844–1882)	first class boy/ seaman	USS *Savannah*						
			USS *Constellation*	09.24.64–09.23.66					
William H. Turner	(1838–05.27.64)	sergeant, No. 1 gun	USS *North Carolina*	04.19.64–05.27.64	Ireland		Rahway Cemetery		
Charles S. Tuttle	(b. 1822)	steward/cook	USS *Nahant*	01.08.62–01.03.63					
George Tuttle	(b. 1836)	seaman	USS *Calypso*	09.04.63–09.30.64	Elizabeth	Negro			
Peter Vanderveer	(b. 1842)	first class boy	USS *Ossipee*						
			USS *Augusta Dinsmore*						
			USS *Mackinaw*	08.01.64–01.31.66			Plainfield		
William H. Vanderveer	(b. 1843)	landsman			Plainfield	Negro			
William van Horn	(d. 08.27.62)	landsman	USS *Suwanee*	01.09.65–05.02.65	Plainfield				

Sailors	B/D	Rank	Vessel(s)	Dates of service	Country of birth	Race	Hometown/ burial site	State credit	Navy Medal
James van Riper	(b. 1845)	first class boy	USS *Grand Gulf*	08.04.63–11.09.65		Negro	Linden		
Owen Vermule	(b. 1832)	landsman	USS *De Soto*						
			USS *Memphis*	08.10.63–09.26.65		black	Plainfield		
Jeremiah F. Voorhees	(1832–10.17.80)	landsman		09.09.64		black	Rahway		
Thomas H. Walker	(1838–05.01.62)	landsman	USS *Monticello*	08.12.61–05.01.62		Negro	Elizabeth		
John Wallace	(b. 1837)	landsman		09.01.64–04.15.65		mulatto	Linden		
Charles Ward	(b. 1838)	seaman	USS *New York*	04.01.65–03.31.68		Negro	Rahway		
John Ward	(1839–07.22.1915)	landsman	USS *New York*	04.01.65–10.01.68		Negro			
George Watson	(b. 1836)	seaman	USS *Ticonderoga*	04.02.63–03.13.65					
			USS *Vanderbilt*	05.27.64–02.16.67			Elizabeth		
Nathaniel Weeks	(1845–1886)	second class boy	USS *Ohio*						
			USS *Richmond*						
			USS *Brooklyn*	10.14.61–11.05.64			Rahway Cemetery		
Charles Williams	(b. 1842)	landsman	USS *Saratoga*	09.19.63–06.30.64					
		seaman		04.28.64	Canada	Negro	Westfield		

Sailors	B/D	Rank	Vessel(s)	Dates of service	Country of birth	Race	Hometown/ burial site	State credit	Navy Medal
John Williams	(1837–03.31.65)	boatswain's mate	USS *Mohican*	11.07.61–07.10.63					
		seaman	USS *Clematis*	09.01.64–08.30.65	Elizabethtown		Evergreen Cemetery, Hillside		✓
William H. Williams	(1836–1911)	landsman	USS *Metacomet*						
			USS *Lehigh*		England	mulatto	Plainfield		✓
Charles Wilson	(b. 1812)	ordinary seaman	USS *North Carolina*	03.09.64–07.05.64	Elizabethtown				
Henry Wilson	(1846–11.27.63)	first class boy		11.17.63–11.27.63	Elizabethtown				
Joseph Wright		landsman	USS *New York*	01.03.65–04.05.67			Elizabeth		
William Zabriski		first class boy	USS *National Guard*	04.22.63–06.30.63		mulatto	Elizabeth		

Appendix D

Sixth New York Independent Battery of Light Artillery, or "Bramhall's Battery"

The Sixth New York Independent Battery of Light Artillery, U.S. Volunteers, was recruited in Rahway and organized in New York City as Artillery Company K of the Ninth New York State Militia and Eighty-third New York Infantry Regiment. It was mustered into service (to serve three years) on June 15, 1861, and served with its regiment until its detachment on August 25, 1861. It was designated by the State of New York as the Sixth Battery. The battery fought exclusively with the Army of the Potomac, attached to the Cavalry Corps as a six-gun horse artillery battery for most of the war. The battery was mustered out on July 8, 1865.

It was commanded originally by Captain Thomas W. Bunting, a mulatto, who was dismissed on December 23, 1861. He was discharged on January 23, 1862, based on an "adverse" report of the examining board. Captain Bunting was succeeded by Rahway's lieutenant Walter Bramhall, who commanded the battery during the Peninsular Campaign where, as Bramhall's Battery, it achieved honorable distinction. Captain Bramhall resigned on February 16, 1863. He was succeeded by Lieutenant Joseph W. Martin, who was honorably discharged at the expiration of his term of service on February 16, 1865. He was succeeded by Lieutenant Moses P. Clark, under whose command the battery returned to Hart's Island, New York Harbor, on July 8, 1865. Soldiers with service in a regiment of the United States Colored Troops are identified with the letters USCT.

Name	B/D	Rank	Dates of service	Hometown	Burial information	Misc.
Watson Antrim	(1836–10.25.1902)	private	09.16.61–09.15.64			
		promoted corporal	03.30.62			
		reduced to private	09.05.63–09.15.64	Rahway		
George W. Bennett	(1842–07.09.62)	private	06.20.61–06.09.62			
		promoted corporal	06.09.62		buried in Section E, Soldiers Plot, Hazelwood Cemetery, Rahway	born in Barbados; died of disease at De Camp General Hospital
William Bishop	(b. 1825)	private	06.20.61–06.19.64			
		promoted corporal	09.20.61–01.09.63			
		sergeant, of No. 1 gun	01.09.63		Rahway Cemetery	wounded, 06.09.63 at Brandy Station, VA
George W. Brandt/Brunt	(b. 1842)	private	04.29.63–07.08.65	Rahway		
Harvey Brandt/Brunt	(1844–05.06.1908)	private	04.29.63–07.08.65		Section G, Plot-Davies-41-Block 37, Hazelwood Cemetery, Rahway	
George Henry Brown Jr.	(1842–04.11.65)	private	06.20.61–06.21.64			
		promoted corporal	03.01.62			
		sergeant	05.24.64			
		first lieutenant	06.21.64	Rahway		died of consumption
George Washington Brown	(1840–1902)	private	08.15.61–01.23.64		buried at Baptist/Methodist Evergreen Cemetery, Plainfield	USCT; discharged for disability at Camp Dickinson, MD

Name	B/D	Rank	Dates of service	Hometown	Burial information	Misc.
David Brooks Clark	(1842–06.27.1906)	private	06.20.61–06.21.64		Rahway Cemetery	USCT
James R. Clark	(b. 1841)	private	09.27.61–09.30.64	Rahway		USCT
Moses P. Clark	(1839–1881)	sergeant	06.20.61–07.08.65			
		sergeant	06.20.61–09.07.61			
		commissioned second lieutenant	01.27.62			
		first lieutenant	05.27.63			
		captain commanding battery	03.22.65	Rahway hometown		prisoner of war, 05.03.63, Chancellorsville, VA
Thomas Crane	(b. 1841)	private	08.15.61–08.16.64	Elizabethtown		captured in action 06.09.63 at Brandy Station, VA; paroled 06.13.64 at City Point, VA; USCT
Samuel E. Day		captain	04.08.64–06.17.65	Rahway		temporarily assigned to battery from Company K, 16th Pennsylvania Cavalry; USCT
William A. Dickerson	(1829–1880)	sergeant		04.15.63		10th NY Light Artillery, 02.25.62–03.01.64; transferred into 6th Independent Battery, NY Light Artillery, 06.22.64–07.08.65
		promoted sergeant	04.15.63			
		quartermaster-sergeant	04.07.65	Rahway		USCT
James Drake	(b. 1843)	private	09.09.61–09.08.64	Rahway		

Name	B/D	Rank	Dates of service	Hometown	Burial information	Misc.
Thomas Ellis	(b. 1841)	private	09.17.61–09.19.64			
		promoted corporal	10.25.62			
		reduced to private		Rahway		dishonorably discharged, 09.19.64 at Washington, D.C., by sentence general court-martial; USCT
Albert T. Freeman	(1844–10.11.83)	private	12.02.61–12.02.64		Rahway Cemetery	wounded and captured at Brandy Station, VA, 06.09.63; paroled, 06.20.63, at City Point, VA; USCT
Uel Freeman	(1836–10.19.1926)	private	06.15.61–01.18.63		Section J, Plot 591, Rahway Cemetery	discharged for disability at camp near Falmouth, VA
James Fulton	(b. 1837)	sergeant, No. 5 gun	06.15.61–10.01.64			
		reduced to private	01.20.63	Rahway		USCT
David A. High	(d. 03.19.97)	private	04.29.63–07.08.65		Section M, Plot 423, Rahway Cemetery	taken prisoner, 06.09.63 at Brandy Station, VA; paroled 06.13.63 at City Point, VA
William H. Hughes	(1819–09.21.1909)	private	08.15.61–08.16.64			
		promoted corporal	09.28.62			
		reduced to private	07.18.64		Section E, David Hughes, Lot 278, Rahway Cemetery	

Name	B/D	Rank	Dates of service	Hometown	Burial information	Misc.
James H. Ingram	(b. 1838)	private	06.20.61–06.21.64			
		promoted corporal	09.01.61			
		sergeant, No. 3 gun	03.01.62			
		first sergeant	06.10.64			
		sergeant	06.21.64			USCT; captured 06.09.63 at Brandy Station, VA; paroled 06.13.63 at City Point, VA
Robert E. Johnson	(b. 1842)	private	08.15.61–08.27.64	Rahway		dishonorably discharged, 08.07.64, at Washington, D.C., by sentence of general court-martial
Charles H. Leonard	(b. 1842)	private	08.15.61–08.16.64	Rahway		
Edwin A. Marsh	(1840–1892)	private	06.20.61–06.21.64		Rahway Cemetery	born in England
Ellis F. Marsh	(b. 1837)	private	09.14.61–09.13.64	Rahway		
William M. Marsh	(1837–1934)	private	09.14.61–09.08.64		Rahway Cemetery	USCT
John W. Martin	(b. 1837)	private	09.27.61–09.30.64			
		promoted bugler		Rahway		
Joseph W. Martin	(1839–11.13.1908)	second lieutenant	06.20.61–06.08.63			
		promoted first lieutenant	06.08.63			
		captain	06.08.63–02.16.65	Rahway	Hazelwood Cemetery, Rahway	

Name	B/D	Rank	Dates of service	Hometown	Burial information	Misc.
Thomas H. McCrossen	(d. 03.15.85)	private	09.23.61–07.08.65			
		promoted corporal	07.01.63			reenlisted 02.13.64
		promoted sergeant				
		quartermaster-sergeant	11.01.64			
		reduced to private	04.07.65		Hazelwood Cemetery, Rahway	
John McDonald	(1840–1894)	private	08.29.61–08.13.64	Rahway	Evergreen Cemetery, Hillside	
Samuel W. McDonald	(b. 1832)	corporal	06.20.61–06.21.64			
		promoted sergeant, no. 6 gun	09.01.63	Rahway		USCT
Cornelius H. Miller	(1842–1888)	private	06.20.61–06.21.64			
		Captain Bramhall's orderly			Hazelwood Cemetery, Rahway	
George W. Moore	(1840–05.06.1919)	private	06.20.61–06.21.64			
		promoted corporal	12.21.63		Section B, Plot 61, Hazelwood Cemetery, Rahway	wounded in action at Brandy Station, VA; USCT
Charles R. Oliver	(1843–07.03.1906)	private	06.20.61–10.64			reenlisted as veteran 02.13.64
		promoted corporal	10.64			
		reduced to private	03.01.65–07.08.65		Rahway Cemetery	USCT

Name	B/D	Rank	Dates of service	Hometown	Burial information	Misc.
James Oliver	(b. 1845)	private	05.09.63–07.08.65		Evergreen Cemetery, Hillside	USCT
Joseph B. Oliver	(1844–05.03.1914)	private	06.20.61–08.18.64			
		promoted corporal	12.23.63		Section C, Plot 125, Rahway Cemetery	wounded in action 06.09.63 at Brandy Station, VA; discharged for wounds at Judiciary Square Hospital, Washington, D.C.; USCT
George M. Plum Jr.	(1842–12.24.1933)	private	06.20.61–03.09.64		Section C, Lot 124, Rahway Cemetery	discharged for disability at Carvers General Hospital, Washington, D.C.
John W. Potter	(1829–01.29.65)	musician	06.20.61–10.9.61	Rahway	Grave 1,002, National Cemetery, Danville, VA	discharged for disability at Poolsville, MD; mulatto
Joseph M. Potter	(1841–1912)	private	08.15.61–12.25.63			
		promoted corporal	09.04.62		Rahway Cemetery	discharged for disability at Campbell Hospital, Washington, D.C.
Theodore F. Randolph	(1837–02.24.82)	private	09.09.61–09.08.64	Rahway		
William H. Randolph	(1831–03.08.1909)	wagoner	06.20.61–06.21.64			
		reduced to private	09.15.64		Section E, Plot 294, Rahway Cemetery	USCT
Archer V. Rossell	(d. 1865)	private		Rahway	National Cemetery, Little Rock, AR	USCT
Jonathan B. Sanders	(b. 1839)	private	06.29.61–06.04.64	Rahway		discharged for disability at De Camp General Hospital, Davids Island, NY; USCT
John W. Simms	(1827–12.12.78)	private	09.09.61–09.08.64		Section E, Plot 235, Rahway Cemetery.	

Name	B/D	Rank	Dates of service	Hometown	Burial information	Misc.
Thompson Thorn	(b. 1841)	private	06.20.61–06.21.64			
		promoted corporal	03.26.62		Hazelwood Cemetery, Rahway	captured in action at Brandy Station, VA 06.09.63; paroled 06.13.63 at City Point, VA
William H. Turner	(1838–05.27.64)	private	06.20.61–05.27.64			
		promoted corporal	09.01.61			
		sergeant	12.21.63		Hazelwood Cemetery, Rahway	wounded in action 05.06.64 at Brockroad, VA; died of amputation of leg at Armory Square, General Hospital; USCT
James H. Williams	(1831–04.08.94)	private	06.22.64–07.08.65		Evergreen Cemetery, Hillside	USCT

Appendix E

Black Soldiers Serving in White Regiments

Often overlooked are Union County and other Northern blacks who served in white regiments. A significant number were foreign-born mulattoes whose racial identification was not easily detected. Many of these soldiers served in regiments of the United States Colored Troops (USCT) and/or the United States Navy and Marine Corps.

Name	Birth-Death	Rank	Company/Regiment	In/Out	Miscellaneous
Henry Abrams	(1826–1907)	private	E 65th NY Infantry	09.01.64–07.17.65	buried at Baptist/Methodist Evergreen Cemetery, Plainfield
Benjamin F. Ackerman		corporal	C 28th NJ Infantry	09.22.62–09.06.63	buried at Evergreen Cemetery, Hillside
George W. Ackerman	(1842–1869)	private	Battery F, 1st Pennsylvania Light Artillery	02.06.64–06.09.65	occupation: painter; Elizabeth resident
Phillip Ackerman	(1843–12.10.1910)	private	B 5th NJ Infantry	02.23.64–11.06.64	
			transferred into E 7th NJ Infantry	11.06.64–07.17.65	buried at Evergreen Cemetery, Hillside
William H. Ackerman	(1841–07.02.63)	private	A 22nd NJ Infantry	09.22.62–02.28.63	
			E 14th Brooklyn/84th NY Infantry	08.25.62–09.17.62	killed at Gettysburg, PA; Elizabeth resident; occupation: laborer; buried in G-22, NY Plot, Gettysburg National Cemetery, PA
Charles A. Adams	(1847–05.20.1913)	private	C 14th NJ Infantry	08.16.62–06.15.65	
			transferred to Veteran Reserve Corps	06.15.64–07.05.65	
			B 11th NJ Infantry	09.21.65–02.25.65	recruit
			transferred to 10th U.S. Infantry	02.25.65–07.31.65	Elizabeth resident; buried at Baptist/Methodist Evergreen Cemetery, Plainfield
Christopher C. Allen	(d. 08.13.1917)	private	A 26th NJ Infantry	11.11.62–06.27.63	buried at Evergreen Cemetery, Hillside

Name	Birth-Death	Rank	Company/Regiment	In/Out	Miscellaneous
John B. Anderson	(1828–03.19.73)	private	K 9th NJ Infantry	01.18.64–07.12.65	
		detailed regimental armorer	A 9th NJ Infantry	09.29.63–04.09.64	recruit; born in Scotland; Elizabeth resident; occupation: blacksmith; buried at Evergreen Cemetery, Hillside
Stewart M. Anderson		private	E 14th NJ Infantry	01.29.64–06.18.65	recruit
			transferred to Company D, 2nd Regiment		Rahway hometown: buried at Rahway Cemetery
Thomas B. Anderson	(1826–1886)	corporal	A 3rd NJ Infantry	09.03.62–06.22.65	recruit; Baptist/Methodist Evergreen Cemetery, Plainfield
Henry Anthony		private	B 27th NJ Infantry	09.19.62–07.02.63	substitute
			B 11th NJ Infantry	09.02.64–06.06.65	recruit
George W. Ash	(d. 1914)	private	D 119th PA Infantry	08.15.62–06.19.65	
			G 9th NJ Infantry	09.30.61–11.23.62	
			K 9th NJ Infantry	03.29.65–07.12.65	recruit; discharged for disability at Newbern, NC; occupation: butcher; Elizabeth resident
Henry Ash		private	K 3rd NJ Infantry	05.10.61–09.17.62	Elizabeth resident

Name	Birth-Death	Rank	Company/Regiment	In/Out	Miscellaneous
George B. Avery	(1843–12.10.1920)	musician	E 14th NJ Infantry	08.26.62–05.04.64	
			Battery D 1st NJ First Artillery	08.31.64–06.17.65	recruit; discharged with disability; buried in Section A, Avery Plot-132, Hazelwood Cemetery, Rahway
James H. Avery	(1825–1898)	private	C 7th NJ Infantry	08.28.61–10.06.62	
			E 14th NJ Infantry	08.26.62–06.18.65	
		corporal		08.12.62	
		sergeant		08.11.62; 06.06.65	discharged for disability at Fort Monroe, VA; born in Scotland; buried at Rahway Cemetery; $100 UC bounty
Thomas Avery	(1847–05.04.72)	private	B 4th NJ Infantry	09.06.64–06.17.65	recruit; buried at Hazelwood Cemetery, Rahway
William H.H. Avery		private	C 30th NJ Infantry	09.17.62–06.27.63	Rahway; $100 UC bounty
Aaron Baker	(d. 1890)	private	G 38th NJ Infantry	09.27.64–06.30.65	Union resident; buried at Methodist Cemetery, Springfield; $300 UC bounty
John C. Baker	(d. 04.21.74)	private	K 9th NJ Infantry	09.29.64–07.10.65	substitute
			K 26th NJ Infantry	09.18.62–06.27.63	buried at Evergreen Cemetery, Hillside.

Name	Birth-Death	Rank	Company/Regiment	In/Out	Miscellaneous
William A. Baker	(d. 08.11.64)	private	F 5th NJ Infantry	08.22.61–09.01.63	
			transferred to Veteran Reserve Corps	09.01.63–06.04.64	taken prisoner near Mountain Run, VA, 11.27.63; Linden resident; died of scurvy at Andersonville, GA; buried in grave 5,379 at National Cemetery, Andersonville, GA
Edward Baldwin Jr.	(d. 04.19.1914)	private	K 9th NJ Infantry	10.15.61–09.18.62	buried in Section A, Plot 105–106, Hazelwood Cemetery, Rahway
Horace Baldwin	(1839–10.24.1900)	corporal	E 26th NJ Infantry	09.18.62–06.27.63	buried in Section P, Plot 9, Grave 1, Center, Evergreen Cemetery, Hillside
John M. Baldwin	(d. 02.09.1902)	private	I 14th NJ Infantry	09.03.64–07.28.65	discharged at Ward Hospital, Newark; buried in Section P, Plot 9, Grave 4 center, Evergreen Cemetery, Hillside
George Bauer	(d. 1864)	private	C 1st NJ Cavalry	11.28.63–04.16.64	Elizabeth resident; died of pneumonia; buried at Military Asylum Cemetery, Washington, D.C.; $300 3rd Ward, Elizabeth bounty
John R. Bennett	(b. 1841)	private	A 22nd NJ Infantry	09.22.62–06.25.63	
William W.R. Bennett	(1836–1898)	private	H 28th NJ Infantry	09.22.62–07.06.63	
			D 4th NJ Infantry	12.05.64–07.09.65	mulatto; occupation: barber; Westfield hometown
Charles Benson	(1839–1881)	private	A 34th NJ Infantry	09.08.64–06.06.65	
		promoted corporal 11.01.64			born in Plainfield

Name	Birth-Death	Rank	Company/Regiment	In/Out	Miscellaneous
Henry C. Brandt	(1840–09.30.1912)		1st Lt. D 54th NY Infantry	09.28.62–03.22.63	resigned 03.20.1863
		captain	16th Infantry, Veteran Reserve Corps		transferred 03.22.63; buried in Evergreen Cemetery, Hillside
Joseph Brandt		private	A 1st NJ Infantry	05.21.61–01.22.63	
		private	I 29th Pennsylvania Infantry	02.04.64–08.03.65	discharged at U.S. Army General Hospital, Philadelphia, PA, for disability; Elizabeth resident
George W. Brill		private	I 8th NJ Infantry	02.25.64–06.13.65	recruit; discharged at Satterlee U.S. Army General Hospital, Philadelphia
George A. Brinkerhoff	(b. 1831)	sergeant	A 22nd NJ Infantry	09.22.62–06.25.63	
		promoted corporal, 09.01.62			
		sergeant, 03.11.63			Westfield resident
John D. Brinkerhoff	(1830–10.24.1911)	private	22nd NJ Infantry	09.22.62–06.25.63	recruit; mulatto; buried at Fairview Cemetery, Westfield
Edwin Brokaw	(1833–1882)	private	C 37th NJ Infantry	06.23.64–10.01.64	Rahway resident; $300 UC bounty
Isaac L. Brokaw	(1840–10.01.97)	corporal	I 3rd NJ Infantry	05.30.61–06.23.64	
		promoted corporal, 03.08.64			
		reduced to rank of private, 03.01.65			occupation: cabinet maker; buried at Baptist/Methodist Evergreen Cemetery, Plainfield

Name	Birth-Death	Rank	Company/Regiment	In/Out	Miscellaneous
Alexander Brown	(1832–1902)	private	B 11th NJ Infantry	06.14.64	substitute
			transferred to Company D		born in Plainfield; buried at Hillside Cemetery, Scotch Plains
Charles M. Brown	(1831–1883)	private	K 9th NJ Infantry	04.12.65–07.12.65	recruit
Henry L. Brown		private	K 9th NJ Infantry	09.30.64–02.24.65	recruit
			transferred to C 9th NJ Infantry	02.24.65–07.12.65	discharged at Ward USA Hospital, Newark, NJ
Milton A. Brown	(d. 11.30.64)	second lieutenant	E 100th Ohio Infantry		
		sergeant		09.01.62–11.30.64	killed at Franklin, TN; buried at Stones River National Cemetery, Murfreesboro, TN; Westfield hometown; removed to Fairview Cemetery, Westfield
James H. Brunt/Brandt	(1842–08.27.1906)	private	I D.C. 2nd Infantry	02.02.62–09.12.65	wounded at Antietam, MD 09.17.62; buried in Section B, Plot 37, Hazelwood Cemetery, Rahway
Thomas Carle	(1832–10.14.63)	private	B 52nd NY Infantry	09.12.63–10.14.63	killed at Bristoe Station, VA; Westfield hometown
Daniel V. Carman	(d. 05.31.62)	musician	H 5th NJ Infantry	08.23.61–05.31.62	died of typhoid fever at Douglass Hospital, Washington, D.C.; buried at Riverview Cemetery, Trenton, NJ
Robert J. Carroll	(1844–01.21.1917)	hospital steward	U.S. Army	11.20.63–10.11.65	
		reduced to private			Elizabeth hometown

Name	Birth-Death	Rank	Company/Regiment	In/Out	Miscellaneous
Edmond D. Chamberlain	(1842–06.21.91)	corporal	E 51st Massachusetts Infantry	09.25.62–07.27.63	
		first sergeant	B Massachusetts Infantry	10.12.64–06.08.65	
		reduced to rank of private, 03.12.64			wounded 11.16.63 at Campbell's Station, TN and at Spotsylvania Courthouse, VA, 05.12.64; occupation: farmer; buried at Fairview Cemetery, Westfield
William Conner Chamberlain	(1843–07.06.1930)	private	D 23rd Massachusetts Infantry	09.28.61–09.02.62	discharged for disability at New Bern, NC; buried in Division 8, Section A, Plot 128, Hillside Cemetery, Scotch Plains
John G. Champion	(d. 10.26.1906)	private	I 12th NJ Infantry	09.04.62–03.16.63	discharged for disability; Elizabeth hometown
William H. Chew		private	D 24th NJ Infantry	09.03.62–06.29.63	
		private	K 9th NJ Infantry	02.23.65–06.12.65	recruit
Isaac Clark	(b. 1840)	corporal	A 3rd NJ Infantry	05.22.61–10.26.62	
		promoted corporal		09.10.61	discharged to enlist in regular U.S. Army; final record unknown; occupation: farmer; Rahway hometown
John R. Clark	(1824–1884)	private	A 22nd NJ Infantry	09.01.62–06.05.63	Linden resident; buried at Rahway Cemetery
Robert Clark	(07.06.18–08.28.89)	private	I 8th NJ Infantry, recruit		buried at Methodist Episcopal Cemetery, New Providence, NJ

Name	Birth-Death	Rank	Company/Regiment	In/Out	Miscellaneous
Thomas Clark	(1842–06.18.65)	private	E 14th NJ Infantry	08.12.62–06.18.65	killed in action at Petersburg, VA; Rahway resident; buried at Fairview Cemetery, Westfield
William H. Cleaveland	(1839–06.30.94)	private	G 8th NY Heavy Artillery	08.14.62–06.09.64	buried at Evergreen Cemetery, Hillside
William H. Cochrane	(1843–06.16.64)	corporal	C 21st NJ Infantry	09.15.62–06.09.63	
		first lieutenant	K 33rd NJ Infantry	08.29.63–06.15.64	
		promoted captain	Company G	05.10.64	killed at Pine Knob, GA; buried at Presbyterian Cemetery, New Providence
Jabez C. Cole	(d. 04.06.1925)	private	I 52nd Pennsylvania Infantry	09.23.61–06.1.62	buried at Evergreen Cemetery, Hillside
Jonathan T. Connett		corporal	H 30th NJ Infantry	09.17.62–06.27.63	buried at Rahway Cemetery
Michael Connolly		private	G 9th NJ Infantry	04.07.65–07.12.65	recruit
Jacob Conover		private	G 9th NJ Infantry	08.16.64–06.14.65	recruit
Samuel S. Conover	(1842–1891)	second lieutenant	C 28th NJ Infantry	09.22.62–07.06.63	buried at Rahway Cemetery
William W. Conover	(1840–1900)	first sergeant	I 14th New York Cavalry	04.25.63–06.12.65	
		promoted quartermaster sergeant			
		sergeant			Elizabeth resident; buried at Evergreen Cemetery, Hillside

Name	Birth-Death	Rank	Company/Regiment	In/Out	Miscellaneous
John Conroy	(d. 02.10.95)	private	K 9th NJ Infantry	10.15.61–12.07.64	Elizabeth; buried at Evergreen Cemetery, Hillside
Alfred Cook	(d. 05.16.64)	private	B 9th NJ Infantry	02.26.64–05.16.64	recruit; killed at Drury's Bluff, VA; Rahway hometown
Charles Cook	(b. 1843)	private	A 9th NJ Infantry	08.20.62–11.17.63	recruit; born in Elizabethtown.
James Cook	(1811–06.28.70)	private	K 9th NJ Infantry	01.18.64–07.12.65	recruit; wounded at Drury's Bluff, VA 05.16.64; Elizabeth hometown; buried at Evergreen Cemetery, Section E–Green, Hillside
Peter Cook	(d. 09.18.64)	private	B 11th NJ Infantry	08.14.62–09.18.64	died of chronic diarrhea at U.S. Army General Hospital, Fort Schuyler, New York Harbor; buried in grave 1902, Cyprus Hill Cemetery, Long Island
William H. Cook	(1843–04.05.1914)	private	K 1st NJ Cavalry	09.01.64–05.08.65	Elizabeth hometown; buried at Evergreen Cemetery, Hillside
James Cooley		private	F 3rd NJ Cavalry	01.12.64–08.01.65	Elizabeth resident
John Corcoran	(1834–1898)	private	K 9th NJ Infantry	09.29.64–06.14.65	substitute
			transferred into F 2nd NJ infantry	06.21.65–07.12.65	recruit; Elizabeth resident
John T. Cox		private	I 25th NJ Infantry	09.26.62–06.20.63	recruit; $300 Linden bounty

Name	Birth-Death	Rank	Company/Regiment	In/Out	Miscellaneous
William H. Cox	(1841–1895)	private	F 11th NJ Infantry	06.15.64–07.06.65	
			D 35th NJ Infantry	02.14.65–06.18.65	born in England; Rahway hometown; buried at Hazelwood Cemetery, Rahway; $300 UC bounty, 12.01.63
Rohan Crite	(d. 06.27.1919)		U.S. Army		buried in Division 3, Section C, Row 5, Single Plot, Colored Adult, Grave 35, Hillside Cemetery, Scotch Plains
Reverend David R. Croshon	(b. 02.15.34)	private	H 141st Ohio Infantry	05.02.64–09.03.64	Elizabeth hometown; $300 1st Ward, Elizabeth bounty
Cornelius Crosson		private	A 1st NJ Infantry	08.13.61–01.22.63	recruit; discharged at Camp Banks, VA, with disability; Rahway hometown
Samuel Crosson	(d. 05.03.97)				buried at Hazelwood Cemetery, Rahway
Thomas H. Crosson	(d. 03.15.85)	corporal	C 30th NJ Infantry	09.17.62–06.27.63	
		reduced to private		10.01.62	buried at Hazelwood Cemetery, Rahway
Jeremiah Crowell	(1830–1875)	private	F 26th NJ Infantry	09.03.62–06.27.63	
		corporal	K 9th NJ Infantry	11.25.63–07.12.65	
		promoted corporal		12.08.64	Rahway hometown; buried at Rahway Cemetery
Joseph Edgar Crowell	(1844–1919)	private	K 13th NJ Infantry	08.25.62–11.15.63	
			transferred into Veteran Reserve Corps	11.15.63–01.29.64	

Name	Birth-Death	Rank	Company/Regiment	In/Out	Miscellaneous
Jeremiah A. Crowley	(1842–01.09.81)	private	M 2nd NJ Cavalry	08.18.64–06.29.65	occupation: machinist/molder; Elizabeth resident; buried at Mt. Olivet Cemetery, Elizabeth
Thomas A. Crowley	(b. 1843)	private	G 9th NJ Infantry	09.30.61–08.18.62	
			F 95th NY Infantry	09.04.63–07.16.65	
		promoted corporal		04.30.64	wounded at Petersburg, VA, 06.18.64; buried at Baptist/Methodist Evergreen Cemetery, Plainfield; $300 1st Ward, Elizabeth bounty
Theodore F. Crowlie	(1844–04.18.1901)	private	E 4th New York Heavy Artillery	12.16.61–01.26.65	occupation: oysterman; born in Germany; Elizabeth resident; buried at Evergreen Cemetery, Hillside
George T. Cummings		private	C 14th NJ Infantry	08.16.62–03.15.64	
			transferred into Veteran Reserve Corps	03.15.64–06.30.65	Elizabeth resident
William Dallas	(d. 03.27.1919)	private	F Pennsylvania 28th Infantry	07.24.63–07.18.65	substitute; buried at Section B, Row 1, Block 51, Fairview Cemetery, Westfield
Francis Davis		corporal	G 9th NJ Infantry	04.11.65–07.12.65	substitute; Elizabeth resident
Joseph H. Davis		private	K 9th NJ Infantry	03.12.64–07.19.65	recruit
Luther A. Davis	(1841–08.20.63)	private	K 9th NJ Infantry	08.21.62–08.20.63	recruit; buried at Evergreen Cemetery, Hillside

Name	Birth-Death	Rank	Company/Regiment	In/Out	Miscellaneous
Daniel Day	(1844–06.23.1906)	private	D 2nd NJ Cavalry	02.17.64–04.17.64	recruit
		private	A 1st Illinois U.S. Light Artillery	10.07.64–07.10.65	occupation: laborer; buried in Lawncrest B, Soldier Plot 88, Grave 112, Evergreen Cemetery, Hillside
David C. Day	(d. 05.14.62)	private	B 8th NJ Infantry	08.29.61–05.04.62	died of wounds at Chesapeake Hospital, Fort Monroe, VA; buried in Section L, Plot 34, Evergreen Cemetery, Hillside
Edward I. Day	(1838–09.09.76)	corporal	K 70th NY Infantry	06.21.61–12.31.63	
		reduced to private		06.08.63	
		corporal	C 86th NY Infantry	12.31.63–06.22.64	reenlisted
		reduced to private		04.15.64	wounded at Gettysburg, PA 07.02.63; buried in Section L, Plot 34, Evergreen Cemetery, Hillside.
Horace H. Day	(1840–02.01.1918)	private	E 25th NJ Infantry	09.18.62–01.12.63	
			F 8th NJ Infantry	02.23.65–07.17.65	buried in Section L, Plot 30, Evergreen Cemetery, Hillside
Mulford B. Day	(d. 04.27.66)	private	C 15th NJ Infantry	08.25.62–04.28.63	buried in Old Division, Methodist Cemetery, New Providence

Name	Birth-Death	Rank	Company/Regiment	In/Out	Miscellaneous
Samuel E. Day		private	K 16th Pennsylvania Cavalry	09.19.62–06.17.65	
			B 9th NJ Infantry 03.29.65, recruit		
			transferred to Company D	03.29.65–07.12.65	recruit; Rahway hometown
William H. Day	(1847–09.08.1926)		B 100th Illinois Infantry		
		private	E 8th NJ Infantry	08.30.61–09.21.64	buried in grave 59-d-5-8, Hillside Cemetery, Scotch Plains
Henry W. De Camp	(b. 1841)	private	L NJ 1st Cavalry	06.12.63–04.21.64	discharged for disability at Newark; occupation: boatman; Elizabeth resident
Charles R. DeGraw	(1831–1898)	private	A 22nd NJ Infantry	09.22.62–06.25.63	Elizabeth resident; buried at Colonel Ledyard Cemetery, Groton, CT
John DeGraw	(d. 1881)	private	K 25th NJ Infantry	09.18.62–06.20.63	recruit; buried in section G, Plot 53-54, Hazelwood Cemetery, Rahway
John W. De Hart	(1841–05.20.73)	private	B 9th NJ Infantry	10.03.64–10.18.65	recruit; occupation: laborer; Elizabeth hometown; buried at Evergreen Cemetery, Hillside
William Chetwood DeHart	(1840–05.23.1922)	private	F 7th NY Infantry	05.25.62–09.05.62	
William A. Dickerson	(1829–1880)	sergeant	10th NY Light Artillery	02.25.62–03.01.64	
		promoted sergeant		04.15.63	Rahway hometown
Charles Dickinson	(d. 06.18.64)	private	I 6th NJ Infantry	12.26.63–06.18.64	killed at battle in Front of Petersburg; buried at Rahway Cemetery
Frederick A. Ditmars	(d. 07.10.1903)	private	C 39th NJ Infantry	10.08.64–06.17.65	recruit; buried in section M, plot 795, Rahway Cemetery

Name	Birth-Death	Rank	Company/Regiment	In/Out	Miscellaneous
John H. Doty	(1844–01.04.1937)	private	K 70th NY Infantry	06.21.61–07.01.64	occupation: farm laborer; Elizabeth hometown; buried at Connecticut Farms Churchyard, Section I, Row L, Union
Samuel K. Doty	(1834–03.29.95)	private	G 9th NJ Infantry	09.30.61–09.30.64	
			transferred to Veteran Reserve Corps		Elizabeth resident; buried in section C, single plot Baptist/Methodist Evergreen Cemetery, Plainfield
Robert J. Douglass		private	K 9th NJ Infantry	03.25.65–07.12.65	recruit
			transferred to Company A		discharged at Ward General Hospital, Newark
Edward S. Dow	(1843–1901)	enlisted corporal	I 5th NY Cavalry	10.31.61	
		second lieutenant	G U.S. Sharpshooters	12.12.61–07.16.62	resigned
			K 14th NY Cavalry	03.30.64–06.29.65	buried at Baptist/Methodist Evergreen Cemetery, Plainfield
George W. Drake	(1842–06.07.65)	corporal	I 15th NJ Infantry	07.28.62–06.22.65	
		promoted corporal		08.01.64	buried in section C, plot 162, grave 1 rear, Evergreen Cemetery, Hillside
Henry C. Drake	(d. 04.26.1928)	private	G 35th NJ Infantry		Plainfield; buried at Hillside Cemetery, Scotch Plains
Jonathan D. Drake	(1841–06.26.1904)	noncommissioned hospital steward	U.S. Army	09.18.62–06.27.63	Elizabeth hometown; buried at Evergreen Cemetery, Hillside

Name	Birth-Death	Rank	Company/Regiment	In/Out	Miscellaneous
Noah W. Drake	(1836–09.25.1911)	private	B 73rd Illinois Infantry		
		private	B 44th Illinois Infantry	10.04.64–06.12.65	buried in Division 8, Section A, Soldiers Plot, Grave 17, Hillside Cemetery, Scotch Plains
Silas Drake	(1824–07.15.1908)	private	C 14th NJ	08.20.64–02.11.65	recruit; discharged at Ward U.S. Army General Hospital, Newark for disability; Elizabeth hometown; buried in Section E, Plot 54, at Evergreen Cemetery, Hillside
William H.B. Drake	(1842–11.17.1902)	private	I 28 NJ Infantry	09.22.62–07.06.63	
		private	Battery D 1st Regiment Artillery	08.31.64–06.17.64	recruit; Plainfield hometown
Edward M. Dubois	(b. 1836)	private	B 14th Rhode Island Heavy Artillery	09.14.63–01.07.65	discharged for disability at Fort Jackson, LA; born in Nassau New Providence; Elizabeth hometown
Abram Dunham	(d. 08.95)	private	D 11th NJ Infantry	08.01.62–08.10.64	
			transferred to Veteran Reserve Corps	08.10.64–07.31.65	buried at Convent United Methodist Church Cemetery, Plainfield
David B. Dunham	(1842–07.01.64)	private	I NY 44th Infantry	09.23.61–07.01.64	
		promoted corporal		08.22.63	
		sergeant		11.01.63	wounded, prisoner of war at Laurel Hill, VA, 05.08.64; died of wounds 07.01.64; Rahway; $300 UC bounty
Enoch W. Dunham	(1845–10.02.63)	private	G 15th Infantry, United States Army		buried at Hazelwood Cemetery, Rahway

Name	Birth-Death	Rank	Company/Regiment	In/Out	Miscellaneous
Jeremiah Dunham	(1843–11.27.63)	private	D 11th NJ Infantry	08.05.62–11.27.63	killed in action at Locust Grove, VA; buried on 04.28.99 in section B, lot 40, Rahway Cemetery
John B. Dunham	(d. 01.18.64)	private	E 14th NJ Infantry	08.09.62–01.18.64	died of chronic diarrhea at Ward U.S. Army General Hospital, Newark, NJ; Rahway hometown
Joseph T. Dunham	(1841–09.12.96)	sergeant	B 78th New York Infantry	10.29.61–08.21.62	
		reduced to rank of private	E 8th New York Heavy Artillery	09.13.63–06.16.65	discharged for disability at Convalescent Camp, VA; wounded 05.03.63 at Chancellorsville, VA; buried in Division 3, Section C, Plot: Row 2, Single Adult, Colored, Grave 60, Hillside Cemetery, Scotch Plains
Randolph Dunham		private	D 11th NJ Infantry	06.30.62–11.15.63	
			transferred to Veteran Reserve Corps	11.15.63–03.09.64	Plainfield hometown
Samuel H. Dunham	(1841–01.26.1902)	first sergeant	A NJ 1st Infantry	05.21.61–07.09.62	discharged for disability
		reduced to private at own request		07.01.61	
		private	C 14th NJ Infantry	09.02.64–06.18.65	recruit; born in Plainfield; buried in Lawncrest B, Soldiers Plot, Grave 24, Evergreen Cemetery, Hillside
William H. Dunham	(1838–01.12.91)	private	E 14th NJ Infantry	08.20.62–09.20.64	discharged at USA Hospital, West Philadelphia, PA, for wounds received in action at Cold Harbor, VA; buried in Section M, Plot 418, Rahway Cemetery

Name	Birth-Death	Rank	Company/Regiment	In/Out	Miscellaneous
George W. Dunn	(d. 03.25.1903)	private	C 26th NJ Infantry	11.11.62–06.27.63	
		promoted corporal		10.10.62	buried in section F, plot 137, Evergreen Cemetery, Hillside
Joseph Dunn	**(1840–06.27.62)**	**private**	**H 7th NJ Infantry**		**occupation: laborer; killed at Gains Farms; $300 1st Ward, Elizabeth bounty; buried at Baptist/Methodist Evergreen Cemetery, Plainfield**
William H. Dunn	(1848–06.30.1900)	second lieutenant	D 10th Michigan Cavalry	11.18.63–11.11.65	
		promoted first lieutenant	Company E	04.25.64	buried at Trinity Churchyard, Woodbridge; $300 1st Ward, Elizabeth bounty, 06.18.63
George Eaton	**(d. 05.08.1925)**	**private**	**C 56th Massachusetts Infantry**		**buried in Lawnplot 3, Plot 297, Grave 1 Front, Evergreen Cemetery, Elizabeth**
Henry C. Ellis	(d. 1901)	corporal	E 35th NJ Infantry	09.18.63–07.20.65	buried at Evergreen Cemetery, Hillside
John Henry Elson	**(1831–1914)**	**private**	**K 31st NJ Infantry**	**09.17.62–06.24.63**	**buried at Evergreen Cemetery, Hillside**
Edward M. Esterbrooks	(1838–12.24.1903)	private	1st Massachusetts Cavalry	12.27.64–06.30.65	
		first sergeant	C 44th NY Infantry	10.05.61–10.25.62	
			transferred to B 44th NY Infantry	10.25.62–10.11.64	
		reduced to private		01.01.62	wounded at Gettysburg, PA on 07.02.63; buried in section A, Plot 126, Grave 3, Evergreen Cemetery, Hillside

Name	Birth-Death	Rank	Company/Regiment	In/Out	Miscellaneous
Charles M. Fay	(1842–1868)	first sergeant	E 101st NY Infantry	12.16.61–01.29.63	wounded at Chantilly, VA, on 09.01.62; discharged for wounds on 01.29.63 at Emory Hospital, Washington, D.C.; Elizabeth hometown; buried at Evergreen Cemetery, Hillside
James W. Fisher	(1843–03.12.81)	sergeant	Battery E, NJ 1st Light Artillery	08.21.63–06.12.64	
		promoted first sergeant		03.28.64	
		second lieutenant		05.28.65	Elizabeth hometown; buried at Evergreen Cemetery, Hillside
George C. Ford		private	G 26th NJ Infantry	09.18.62–06.27.63	Linden resident
Isaac Forman	(1841–1890)	private	C 35th Pennsylvania Infantry	07.15.61–05.08.64	listed as wounded at Spotsylvania Courthouse, VA; buried at Evergreen Cemetery, Hillside
John P. Fox		private	H 10th NY Heavy Artillery	10.03.65–10.03.68	Elizabeth hometown; buried in Plot 258, Block G, Grave D, Mt. Olivet Cemetery, Elizabeth
John C. Francis	(1845–07.31.89)	private	I 2nd Massachusetts Heavy Artillery	12.11.63–09.03.65	buried in Section D, Soldier Plot 87, Grave 14, Evergreen Cemetery, Hillside
John T. Frank	(1814–1883)	private	H 9th NJ Infantry	08.30.64–06.14.65	substitute; discharged at Greensboro, NC; occupation: blacksmith; Elizabeth hometown; buried at Evergreen Cemetery, Hillside
Charles P. Freeman	(1841–06.08.1914)	first sergeant	H 31st NJ Infantry	09.17.62–06.24.63	
		corporal	B 39th NJ Infantry	09.30.64–06.17.65	buried in Section J, Plot 59, Rahway Cemetery

Name	Birth-Death	Rank	Company/Regiment	In/Out	Miscellaneous
Enos E. Freeman	(1826–01.14.79)	private	G 15th NJ Infantry		buried in Section M, Grave 87, Rahway Cemetery
Thomas Freeman	(1841–11.11.62)	private	K 9th NJ Infantry	10.15.61–03.14.62	discharged at USA Hospital, Fortress Monroe on account of wounds received in action at Newbern, NC; died at Chesapeake General Hospital, Fortress Monroe, Virginia; mulatto; born in Lodi, NJ
Henry Frost	(b. 1835)	corporal	H 10th NJ Infantry	06.02.62–07.31.64	Westfield hometown
John R. Fulton	(b. 1837)	sergeant	A 22nd NJ Infantry	09.22.62–06.25.63	
		reduced to private		01.20.65	
Thomas Gallagher	(d. 11.19.1906)	captain	H 150th NY Infantry	08.07.63–06.07.65	Linden; buried at Evergreen Cemetery, Elizabeth
James K. Giles	(b. 1842)	corporal	C 14th NJ Infantry	08.26.62–06.18.65	
		promoted corporal		05.01.65	
William Godfrey	(d. 07.07.92)	private	E 169th NY Infantry	01.26.64–06.16.65	discharged on surgeon certificate; Elizabeth hometown; buried at Evergreen Cemetery, Hillside
Samuel Godshalk	(d. 05.23.1907)	private	B 104th Pennsylvania Infantry	09.15.61–09.30.64	
		corporal		05.09.62	
		reduced to private		01.05.63	buried in Section H, Row 1, Block 26, Grave 2, Fairview Cemetery, Westfield

Name	Birth-Death	Rank	Company/Regiment	In/Out	Miscellaneous
George Goodwin	(1821–04.17.98)	private	I 3rd NJ Infantry	05.30.61 09.24.62	
		private	D 35th NJ Infantry	02.16.65–06.21.65	buried at Fairview Cemetery, Westfield
George P. Gould		corporal	C 9th NJ Infantry	09.10.61–07.31.63	
		reduced to private	A 10th NJ Infantry, reenlisted	11.25.63–07.12.65	recruit; Linden resident
William J. Gould	(b. 1843)	private	F 26th NJ Infantry	09.03.62–06.27.63	born in Jamaica; Rahway hometown
Joseph Grace		private	A 1st Connecticut Heavy Artillery	05.22.61–05.21.64	Elizabeth hometown; buried at Mt. Olivet Cemetery, Elizabeth
Robert Graham	(1823–11.01.99)	private	A 9th NJ Infantry	03.25.65–07.12.65	recruit; Linden; buried in Section Lawncrest B, Soldier Plot 88, Grave 72, Evergreen Cemetery, Scotch Plains
Samuel K. Green	(1845–07.26.64)	artificer	A 1st NY Engineers	09.19.64–07.03.65	
		promoted artificer		06.01.65	buried in Division 3, Section C, Row 3 Colored adult, Grave 27, Hillside Cemetery, Scotch Plains
John Gregory		private	F 28th NJ Infantry	09.22.62–07.06.63	Linden resident
Thomas R. Gregory		private	A 15th NJ Infantry	08.25.62–06.22.65	Linden resident

Name	Birth-Death	Rank	Company/Regiment	In/Out	Miscellaneous
Francis Hall		sergeant	A 1st NJ Infantry	05.16.61–05.23.63	
		reduced to private		11.01.62	discharged for disability at Convalescent Camp, Alexandria, VA; Elizabeth resident
George B. Hall	(1845–10.15.1917)	private	D 25th NJ Infantry	09.26.62–03.06.63	discharged for disability at Armory Square Hospital, Washington, D.C.
			transferred to 9th NJ Veteran Reserve Corps	01.20.64–09.23.64	buried in Soldiers Plot, Evergreen Cemetery, Hillside
James Hall	(1840–09.20.84)	private	E 15th NJ Infantry		
			E 2nd NJ Infantry		
			E 28th NJ Infantry		buried in Old Public Grounds, Colored Map-1, Row 2 Adult, Grave 26, Evergreen Cemetery, Hillside
Edward Scott Hand		private	E 14th NJ Infantry	02.24.65–06.18.65	recruit
			transferred to D 2nd NJ Infantry	06.18.65–07.11.65	recruit; Linden resident
Enoch W. Hand	(b. 1839)	private	K 2nd Michigan Infantry	04.14.64–03.04.65	
			transferred Veteran Reserve Corp	03.04.65–07.28.65	discharged for wounds; Plainfield hometown
Henry Wells Hand	(1841–1905)	private	F 136th NY Infantry	09.25.62–03.31.64	buried in New Section, Plot 38, Row 4, Grave 2, Scotch Plains Baptist Church Cemetery

Name	Birth-Death	Rank	Company/Regiment	In/Out	Miscellaneous
James Hand	(d. 01.29.65)	private	G 9th NJ Infantry	09.30.61 11.05.65	enlisted at 16 years old, Elizabeth hometown
Jesse G. Hand	(d. 11.08.64)	private	E 14th NJ Infantry	08.15.62–11.08.64	died of diarrhea at Rebel prison, Danville, VA; buried at Danville Cemetery, VA
John Hand	(1831–08.31.61)	corporal	I 3rd Infantry	05.30.61–08.31.61	killed in skirmish at Munson Hill, VA; buried in New Section, Plot 38, Row 4, Gravel, Scotch Plains Baptist Church Cemetery
William C. Hand	(d. 02.14.1916)	private	B 11th NJ Infantry	08.11.62–06.06.65	
		promoted sergeant		02.01.63	
		first sergeant		07.01.63	
			transferred to I 11th NJ Infantry, 10/21/64		
		promoted second lieutenant			
		reduced to private			Plainfield hometown; buried at Brooke Avenue Presbyterian Churchyard Cemetery, North Plainfield
John H. Harvey	(1838–06.23.1905)	sergeant	E 14th NJ Infantry	08.12.62–06.18.65	buried in Section M, Plot 791, Rahway Cemetery
Jacob Hedden	(1837–05.03.63)	private	I 8th NJ Infantry	09.13.61–05.03/63	killed at Chancellorsville, VA; mulatto; Rahway resident

Name	Birth-Death	Rank	Company/Regiment	In/Out	Miscellaneous
William Hedden	(1831–05.17.63)	private	I 3rd NJ Infantry	05.27.61–05.17.63	
		promoted sergeant		10.25.62	gunshot wound of spine at Salem Heights, VA, 05.03.63; died at Stanton Hospital, Washington, D.C.; buried at Military Asylum Cemetery, Washington, D.C.; buried 02.16.1913, Division 2, Section A, Plot 57, Hillside Cemetery, Scotch Plains
Henry Henry	(1830–1880)	cook	A 162nd NY Infantry	02.17.64–03.28.64	recruit; Elizabeth resident. $300 UC bounty, 03.19.63
John Lewis Henry	(1836–06.29.65)	private	C 14th NJ Infantry	08.16.62–02.10.63	
			transferred to B 132nd NY Infantry	09.10.63–06.29.65	died of disease at Bachellors Creek, VA; $300 UC bounty, 03.27.63
Thomas Henry	(1832–1883)	private	D 3rd NJ Cavalry	12.02.63–02.18.64	Plainfield hometown; $250 UC bounty, 01.09.63
William Henry	(1842–04.26.1906)	private	C 14th NJ Infantry	08.26.62–05.29.65	discharged at Mower General Hospital, Philadelphia, PA, by order of War Department; born in British North America; Elizabeth resident; buried in Lawncrest B, Soldiers Plot 88, Grave 111, Evergreen Cemetery, Hillside
David S.C. Higgins Jr.	(1843–1865)	corporal	K 9th NJ Infantry	10.15.61–12.07.64	
		promoted corporal		05.26.63	boarder in Elizabeth; buried at Evergreen Cemetery, Hillside
Thomas Higgins	(1824–11.18.95)	private	H 22nd NJ Infantry	09.22.62–06.25.63	buried in Block B, Mt. Oliver Cemetery, Elizabeth

Name	Birth-Death	Rank	Company/Regiment	In/Out	Miscellaneous
William E. Hill	(1838–02.01.1913)	corporal	G 6th Massachusetts Infantry	08.31.62 06.03.63	
			transferred to 15th Massachusetts Light Artillery	12.04.63–01.04.65	
			transferred into 6th Massachusetts Light Artillery	01.04.65–08.07.65	Elizabeth; buried in Lawncrest B, Soldiers Plot, Evergreen Cemetery, Hillside
John Hoff	(d. 1905)	sergeant	A 31st NJ Infantry		buried in Division 23, Oak Drive Section, Plot 20, Presbyterian Cemetery, Springfield
Abraham Holland	(d. 12.16.64)	captain	C 30th NJ Infantry	09.17.62–06.27.63	
		captain		09.15.62	buried at Beauford Cemetery, SC; Westfield resident
George L. Holland	(1842–1909)	private	L NJ 1st Cavalry	10.07.64–07.24.65	
			transferred to D NJ 1st Cavalry		buried at Fairview Cemetery, Westfield
John M. Holston		corporal	K 9th NJ Infantry	02.24.65–06.12.65	recruit
		promoted corporal		06.15.65	
		transferred corporal	G 9th NJ	06.15.65–07.12.65	
James Frank Hubbard	(d. 03.07.1905)	captain	H 30th NJ Infantry		buried in Division 5, Section A, Plot 99, Hillside Cemetery, Scotch Plains

Name	Birth-Death	Rank	Company/Regiment	In/Out	Miscellaneous
Hugh Hughes	(d. 06.03.1917)	private	A 2nd NJ Infantry	05.04.61–06.21.64	
		first sergeant	D 40th NJ Infantry	01.26.65–07.25.65	
		reduced to private		04.08.65	buried in Section E, David Hughes's Lot 278, Rahway Cemetery
Jacob Hunt		private	E 30th NJ Infantry	09.17.62–06.27.63	
		captain	A 1st Battalion	11.14.64–06.29.65	
James C. Hunt		private	G 4th Regiment Cavalry/64th Pennsylvania		
			I 1st NJ Calvary, 8/15/61		
		first lieutenant		02.17.62	
		second lieutenant	1st United States Army, 1st Cavalry, 2/19/62		
		quartermaster		07.18.62	
		sergeant		01.01.64	
		captain		06.28.64	border, Elizabeth
Thomas R. Hunt		first sergeant	A 5th NJ Infantry	08.14.61–11.06.64	
			transferred to G, 08.11.62		
		reduced to private			wounded in action at Chancellorsville, VA on 05.02.63; Rahway hometown

Name	Birth-Death	Rank	Company/Regiment	In/Out	Miscellaneous
Jacob L. Hutt		musician	4th NJ Infantry	10.10.61–08.09.62	
		first lieutenant	C 4th NY Infantry	11.14.64–06.04.65	
John K. Jackson		private	K 9th NJ Infantry	09.29.64–06.14.65	recruit
Thomas R. Jackson	(1818–07.03.97)	private	H 3rd NJ Infantry, substitute		
			F 4th NJ Infantry		Rahway born; buried Section M, Grave 221, Rahway Cemetery
William H. Jackson	(b. 1835)	private	D 11th NJ Infantry, 07.02.62		
			D 43rd Pennsylvania, 1st Light Artillery	08.17.63–08.17.64	Elizabeth hometown
David B. Jenkins	(1840–03.10.81)	corporal	F 91st NY Infantry corporal	11.11.61–09.10.63	discharged for promotion and commission into the Corps d' Afrique, 09.10.63; buried in Section L, Plot 80, Grave 2, Evergreen Cemetery, Hillside
Edward Jewell	(b. 1843)	private	I 8th NJ Infantry	12.24.61–02.23.63	recruit; wounded at Williamsburg by musket ball fracturing both bones of the right leg near their articulation at the knee on 05.05.62; discharged at U.S. Army General Hospital, PA, 02.23.63; disability; Rahway hometown
John H. Johnson	(1840–07.13.63)	private	H 5th NJ Infantry	08.23.61–07.03.63	missing in action at Gettysburg, PA, 07.03.63, recorded at pension office as died that day; listed on Samuel Johnson's stone at Rahway Cemetery

Name	Birth-Death	Rank	Company/Regiment	In/Out	Miscellaneous
John L. Johnson	(1844–05.09.83)	private	H 1st NJ Infantry, recruit, 01.10.62		
		private	G 9th NJ Infantry	04.10.65–07.12.65	drafted; $250 UC bounty
William H. Johnson	(b. 1840)	private	G 9th NJ Infantry	09.30.64–06.14.65	substitute
		promoted corporal		11.01.64	
William M. Johnson	(1844–05.22.1908)	private	K 9th NJ Infantry	02.24.65–07.12.65	recruit
			transferred to Company C		buried in Plot 18 C, Grave 1, Scotch Plains Baptist Cemetery, Scotch Plains
Albert G. Jones	(1841–1875)	sergeant	H 1st NY Engineers	12.07.61–12.06.64	buried at Rahway Cemetery
Edward C. Jones	(1844–1910)	musician	C 14th NJ Infantry	08.26.62–06.18.65	Plainfield hometown
Obadiah F. Jones	(d. 01.31.1917)	sergeant	E 14th NJ Infantry	08.12.62–06.18.65	
		reduced to private		12.01.64	buried in Section A, Plot 18, Hazelwood Cemetery, Rahway
William A. Jones	(1825–12.20.90)	private	Battery B, NJ Light Artillery; C 14th NJ Infantry	09.06.64–06.18.65	buried in Baptist/Methodist Evergreen Cemetery, Plainfield
John Kane	(d. 06.25.65)	private	K 9th NJ Infantry	12.28.64–06.26.65	substitute; died of typhoid fever at Carver U.S. Army General Hospital, Washington, D.C.; buried in grave 5700 at Arlington Cemetery, VA; reinterred 2/6/1906, Block G–198, Grave D, Mt. Olivet Cemetery, Elizabeth

Name	Birth-Death	Rank	Company/Regiment	In/Out	Miscellaneous
Josiah Kellum		private	K 9th NJ, 03.28.65		
			transferred A 9th NJ Infantry	03.28.65–07.12.65	recruit; Linden resident
Henry C. Kent		private	D 11th NJ Infantry	08.08.62–06.06.65	
			transferred to C 11th NJ Infantry		wounded in action at the Battle of Fredericksburg, VA; Rahway hometown
Daniel Kennedy		corporal	G 9th NJ Infantry	10.01.64–06.14.65	substitute
		promoted corporal	Linden resident	05.24.65	
Francis Kennedy	(d. 04.03.1924)	private	C 42nd NY Infantry	06.01.61–06.64	buried in Section Wilbur, Plot 217, Grave 3, Rosedale Cemetery, Linden
Joseph H. King	(1845–07.31.64)	private	H 9th NJ Infantry	03.07.62–12.16.62	recruit; wounded at Whitehall, NC; reenlisted
		second lieutenant	A 35th New Jersey Infantry	03.18.64–07.12.64	died at Carrolton, LA; mulatto; born in Lisbon, Portugal; Rahway hometown
George W. Kinsey	(d. 1884)	corporal	C 30th NJ Infantry	09.17.62–06.27.63	
			D 13th NJ Infantry	08.25.62–06.08.65	buried in Section A, Plot Kinsey–119, Hazelwood Cemetery, Rahway
Peter Kinsey		private	A 26th NJ Infantry	09.18.62–06.27.63	
			A 13th NJ Infantry	09.01.64–05.04.65	substitute; Linden resident

Name	Birth-Death	Rank	Company/Regiment	In/Out	Miscellaneous
William Baker Kinsey		corporal	B 161st NY Infantry	09.16.62–09.20.65	
		corporal	G 40th NJ Infantry	02.14.65–07.13.65	Linden resident
Charles P. Layton	(1846–10.19.64)	private	A 14th NJ Infantry	08.07.62–10.19.64	killed in action at Cedar Creek, VA; Plainfield hometown; given governmental burial in section G, single grave, Methodist/Baptist Evergreen Cemetery, Plainfield
Samuel Layton	(d. 12.10.99)	private	M 2nd NJ Cavalry	08.16.64–06.29.65	buried in section 10, Plot 14, Baptist/Methodist Evergreen Cemetery, Plainfield
John Lee	(d. 1836)	private	E 14th NJ Infantry	08.01.62–11.13.63	discharged at Mt. Pleasant Hospital, Washington, D.C.; disability; Elizabeth resident
Peter Lee		private	D 3rd NJ Cavalry	12.02.63–03.30.64	Elizabeth hometown
Henry H. Leeds	(d. 08.21.1915)	private	6th Pennsylvania Cavalry	11.12.64	buried at Evergreen Cemetery, Hillside
William W. Littell	(1843–05.24.63)	private	G 3rd NJ Infantry	05.29.61–05.04.63	wounded at Salem Heights, VA, on 05.03.63; died of wounds received in action at Salem Heights, VA; government burial section 1, Plot 2, Baptist/Methodist Evergreen Cemetery, Plainfield
Henry A. Little		private	F 29th NJ Infantry	09.20.62–07.06.63	Westfield hometown; $300 UC bounty, 06.18.63

Name	Birth-Death	Rank	Company/Regiment	In/Out	Miscellaneous
Isaac S. Little	(d. 02.21.1929)	private	K 9th NJ Infantry	03.03.65 07.12.65	recruit
			transferred to Company F		prisoner of war, Wilderness, VA, 05.05.64; confined at Macon, GA; returned 03.01.65; buried in Section C, Lot 11-Block 31, Grave 3, Hollywood Cemetery, Union
Jacob Little	(d. 06.01.64)	private	E 14th NJ Infantry	08.26.62–06.01.64	killed at Cold Harbor, VA; buried in Section A, National Cemetery, Cold Harbor, VA
James A. Little	(d. 12.27.1924)	private	E 14th NJ Infantry	08.15.62–06.18.65	
		sergeant	F 19th U.S. Army Infantry		buried in Section F, Plot 213, Evergreen Cemetery, Hillside
John W. Long		first sergeant	E 14th NJ Infantry	08.15.62–06.06.63	
		reduced to private		02.01.63	Rahway hometown
William Long		private	C 9th NJ Infantry	08.04.62–06.14.65	recruit
			G 7th NJ Infantry	11.12.63–05.29.65	Rahway hometown; $300 UC bounty
Marshall Love		private	K 39th NJ Infantry	09.23.64–06.17.65	Elizabeth
William Henry Manning	(b. 1843)	private	A 123rd NY Infantry	09.04.62–06.08.65	
		promoted corporal		01.01.63	wounded at Chancellorsville, VA, on 05.03.63; born in Plainfield

Name	Birth-Death	Rank	Company/Regiment	In/Out	Miscellaneous
Charles G. Marsh	(1844–01.12.1921)	private	Battery H, 4th NY Heavy Artillery	08.06.62–07.20.65	
		second lieutenant	G 39th NJ Infantry	09.23.64–06.17.65	Elizabeth born; buried at Evergreen Cemetery, Hillside
Clarence W. Marsh	(b. 1842)	private	A 8th Massachusetts Infantry	04.30.61–08.01.61	
		mariner		11.17.61–12.25.63	Rahway hometown; $300 UC bounty
Joseph N. Marsh	(d. 02.19.65)	private	E 14th NJ Infantry	02.12.64–02.19.65	died of diarrhea at Rebel prison, Danville, VA; buried at National Cemetery, Danville, VA
Joseph R. Marsh	(d. 12.09.75)	bugler	K 1st NJ Cavalry	12.21.63–07.24.65	
		promoted bugler		06.20.65	discharged at Slough hospital, Alexandria, VA; buried in Section D, Plot 89, Evergreen Cemetery, Elizabeth
Randolph Marsh	(1832–1915)	second lieutenant	C 2nd NJ Infantry		occupation: mason; buried in section 4, Plot 182, Baptist/Methodist Evergreen Cemetery, Plainfield
Robert Marsh	(1844–1914)	corporal	D 20th Massachusetts Volunteers Infantry		
			F 86th NY Infantry		
			G 136th NY Infantry		buried at Hillside Cemetery, Scotch Plains
Silas H. Marsh	(d. 07.30.64)	corporal	C 30th NJ Infantry		buried in Section F, Plot 67 Rahway Cemetery; $300 3rd Ward, Elizabeth UC bounty 06.18.63

Name	Birth-Death	Rank	Company/Regiment	In/Out	Miscellaneous
Solomon H. Marsh		private	I 8th NJ Infantry	09.03.61–12.19.62	wounded in action; discharged at Baltimore, MD, with disability; Rahway hometown
Stephen H. Marsh	(d. 11.13.1919)	first lieutenant	L NJ Infantry		
		first lieutenant		09.22.62–07.02.63	
		first lieutenant		09.02.62	
		second lieutenant	C 40th NJ Infantry	03.02.65–07.13.65	mustered out at Hall's Hill, VA; buried in Lawnplot-3, Block 5, Plot 377, Grave 2 Rear, Evergreen Cemetery, Hillside; $300 UC bounty, 08.08.64
William G. Marsh	(1825–06.01.80)	private	C 23rd Illinois Infantry		
		corporal	C 30th NJ Infantry	09.17.62–06.27.63	
		reduced to private		02.25.63	buried in Section 1, Row 19, Methodist Cemetery, New Providence
William I. Marsh	(1831–07.28.1920)	musician	B 3rd NJ Infantry	09.17.62–06.22.65	Elizabeth resident; buried in Lawnplot 1 Section, Plot 121, Grave 2-Front, Evergreen Cemetery, Hillside; $300 UC bounty
William R. Marsh	(1837–1934)	private	E 14th New Jersey Infantry	09.06.64–06.18.65	recruit; buried at Rahway Cemetery
John V. Martin	(d. 11.26.98)	corporal	C 14th NJ Infantry	08.26.62–06.18.65	
		promoted corporal		12.01.64	Elizabeth; buried in section E, Plot 113, Grave 3-rear, Evergreen Cemetery, Hillside

Name	Birth-Death	Rank	Company/Regiment	In/Out	Miscellaneous
William B. Mason	(1845–12.23.1916)	corporal	I 9th Connecticut Infantry	10.01.61–10.12.64	
			reenlisted, D 9th Connecticut	10.12.64–08.03.65	
		reduced to private			buried in Lawncrest D Section, Soldier Plot 88, Grave 13, Evergreen Cemetery, Hillside
Henry T. Maxwell		private	K 9th NJ Infantry	04.13.65–07.12.65	recruit
			transferred to Company E		
Reverend Thomas C. Mayham	(1841–11.08.1915)	private	4th NY Heavy Artillery; E 6th Kentucky Cavalry	12.24.61–12.19.62	buried in Lawncrest A, Plot 333, Grave 2-Front, Evergreen Cemetery, Hillside
Edward H. Maynard	(1838–1909)	private	D 185th NY Infantry	09.19.64–05.30.65	occupation: barber; buried in Division 5, Section C, Row 8–S.C.A., Grave 26, Hillside Cemetery, Scotch Plains
John McDonald	(1840–1894)	corporal	G 9th NJ Infantry	03.08.65–07.12.65	recruit
		corporal	F 12th Pennsylvania Cavalry	05.19.64–03.08.65; 07.01.65	born in Ireland; Rahway resident; buried at Evergreen Cemetery, Hillside; $300 Rahway bounty
Henry McFarland		private	I 8th NJ Infantry	10.14.61–12.11.62	discharged to join regular U.S. Army; Rahway hometown
James McKinney	(d. 01.26.86)	private	C 19th NY Infantry		buried in Section D, Soldiers Plot 87, Grave 82, Evergreen Cemetery, Hillside
John L. Miller	(d. 01.30.1917)	private	H 5th NJ Infantry	10.28.62–07.18.63	recruit; buried at Fairview Cemetery, Westfield
John V. Miller	(d. 08.27.62)	private	A 1st NJ Infantry	05.16.61–08.27.62	killed in action at Manassas, VA

Name	Birth-Death	Rank	Company/Regiment	In/Out	Miscellaneous
Cornelius Morris	(b. 1842)	private	B 177th NY Infantry	11.21.62–09.10.63	
		corporal	A 178th NY Infantry	06.18.63–03.31.66	
		reduced to private		08.31.64	born at Elizabeth Port
Joseph E. Morse Jr.	(d. 02.11.1921)	private	K 39th Infantry	09.23.64–06.17.65	buried in Division 2, Section D, Plot 146–Row 11, Hillside Cemetery, Scotch Plains
William Morse		private	F 3rd NJ Cavalry	08.30.64–06.06.65	recruit
			transferred from Company G		Linden resident
Isaac Mulford		private	A 3rd NJ Calvary	01.26.64–08.01.65	
		corporal		06.11.64	Received $300 UC bounty
John K. Mulford		private	B 10th NJ Infantry		
			C 7th NJ Infantry		Linden resident; $300 UC bounty; Linden resident
Charles Mulligan		private	E 26th NJ Infantry	09.18.62–06.27.63	Linden resident
John F. Murray	(b. 1840)	private	K 9th NJ Infantry	03.28.65–07.12.65	recruit
			intra regimental company transfer from Company K to Company G		

Name	Birth-Death	Rank	Company/Regiment	In/Out	Miscellaneous
Samuel Murray	(d. 03.24.1901)	wagoner	G 9th NJ Infantry	09.30.61–07.26.65	
		reduced to private		01.01.64	reenlisted 01.18.64; buried in Lawncrest B, Soldiers Plot 88, Grave 68, Evergreen Cemetery, Hillside
Thomas Murray	(d. 05.28.63)	private	E 11th NJ Infantry	06.17.62–05.28.63	died at U.S. Army General Hospital, Washington, D.C., of wounds received in action at Chancellorsville, VA, 05.03.63; buried at Military Asylum Cemetery, Washington, D.C.
James H.C. Nelson	(b. 1841)	private	C 26th NJ Infantry	09.18.62–06.27.63	
			K 9th NJ Infantry	02.24.65–07.12.65	recruit; Westfield hometown
William H. Newbern	(d. 06.08.65)	private	K 9th NJ Infantry	02.23.65–06.8.65	recruit
			transferred to Company A		died at Finley U.S. Army General Hospital, Washington, D.C.
Dallas Noe		private	H 5th NJ Infantry	08.23.61–10.26.62	discharged to enlist in regular army
			A 2nd U.S. Calvary, 10.27.62		Rahway hometown
Elmer Noe	(d. 06.01.64)	private	E 14th NJ Infantry	08.04.62–06.01.64	killed in action at Cold Harbor, VA; Linden resident
Smith H. Noe	(1820–1889)	private	H 5th NJ Infantry	09.21.61–09.07.64	Linden resident; buried at Rahway Cemetery; $300 UC bounty

Name	Birth-Death	Rank	Company/Regiment	In/Out	Miscellaneous
Henry W. Nutt	(d. 06.12.64)	private	G 9th NJ Infantry	02.13.64–06.12.64	recruit; killed in action from minnie ball entering forehead at Cold Harbor, VA; buried in section C, Cold Harbor National Cemetery, VA
Jeremiah Oliver		cook	B 1st Battalion, NJ Infantry	01.05.64–06.29.65	Plainfield resident
Samuel M. Oliver	(d. 01.24.1905)	private	I 2nd District of Columbia Infantry	02.29.64–09.12.65	buried Section J, Outside of Oliver Vault, Rahway Cemetery
William H. Olmstead	(b. 1839)	private	H 2nd NY Heavy Artillery	12.28.63–06.29.65	Rahway resident
Edward C. Parker	(b.1843)	private	G 23rd NJ Infantry	08.25.62–06.27.63	Linden resident
James E. Parker	(b. 1842)	private	B 9th NY Heavy Artillery	12.29.63–06.27.65	born in Norway; mulatto; occupation: farmer; buried at Rahway Cemetery
John Parker	(b. 1844)	private	K 9th NJ Infantry	02.23.65–07.12.65	recruit
			transferred to Company A		Elizabeth resident
William H. Patterson		private	F 28th NJ Infantry	09.22.62–07.06.63	$300 Rahway bounty, 03.29.63
Frederick G. Peach	(d. 06.07.64)		G 9th NJ Infantry	02.08.64–07.07.64	recruit; wounded in left side at Swift Creek, 05.10.64; died at Point of Rocks, MD; Elizabeth hometown; buried in Grave 12,772, Arlington Cemetery, VA
John Peacock	(b. 1835)	private	K 9th NJ Infantry	03.07.65–07.12.65	recruit
Nathan C. Pennington	(1940–11.22.1919)	private	C 28th NJ Infantry	09.22.62–07.06.63	buried in Division 4, Section A, Plot 127, Hillside Cemetery, Scotch Plains

Name	Birth-Death	Rank	Company/Regiment	In/Out	Miscellaneous
John Perkins		private	D 34th NJ Infantry	01.16.65	recruit; Linden
James P. Phillips	**(d. 05.05.62)**	**corporal**	**I 8th NJ Infantry**	**09.13.61–05.05.62**	**killed in action at Williamsburg, VA; Rahway hometown**
Jacob Post	(b. 1831)	first lieutenant	A 22nd NJ Infantry	09.22.62–06.25.63	
		promoted adjutant		01.01.63	
David M. Potter	**(1815–1879)**	**private**	**E 107th NY Infantry**	**07.22.62–09.29.62**	
		private	**E 14th NJ Infantry**	**08.01.62–04.28.63**	**Union resident**
Edward C. Potter Sr.	(1836–1907)	private	C 173rd NY Infantry	01.05.64–10.25.64	buried at Rahway Cemetery
George L. Potter	**(b. 1844–07.02.64)**	**private**	**G 117th NY Infantry**	**01.02.64–07.02.64**	**died of wounds on hospital boat *Monitor***
George N. Potter	(1820–07.05.1919)	sergeant	A 2nd NJ Infantry	08.23.61–06.01.64	
		promoted sergeant		02.25.63	mulatto; Elizabeth; buried in Lawnplot 1, Plot 149, Grave 2–Front, Evergreen Cemetery, Hillside
Henry L. Potter	**(d. 03.29.1907)**	**private**	**K 7th NJ Infantry**	**02.28.65–07.02.65**	**substitute; Linden; buried in Section M, Plot 582, Rahway Cemetery**
John W. Potter	(1829–01.29.65)	private	K 14th NJ Infantry	08.26.62–10.19.64	
			transferred to F		wounded at Cedar Creek, VA; died of pneumonia as a prisoner of war at Rebel prison, Danville, VA; buried in grave 1,002, National Cemetery, Danville, VA

Name	Birth-Death	Rank	Company/Regiment	In/Out	Miscellaneous
William E. Potter	(1840–1896)	second lieutenant	K 12th NJ Infantry	09.01.62 03.03.64	
		transferred; captain	G 12th NJ Infantry	03.03.64–07.15.65	substitute; Linden resident; buried at Old Broad Street Presbyterian Church, Bridgeton, Cumberland County
William H. Powell	(b. 1845)	private	A 1st NJ Cavalry	12.22.63–07.24.65	
		promoted sergeant		03.01.65	
		second lieutenant		07.18.65	
Charles Powers		private	F 83rd NY Infantry	08.28.63–06.23.64	Linden resident
John S. Powers	(1842–10.09.1922)	private	B 11th NJ Infantry	08.19.62–09.01.63	
			transferred to Veteran Reserve Corps	09.01.63–06.28.65	occupation: barber; Plainfield resident
William H. Powers	(1828–1879)	corporal	G 13th New Hampshire Infantry	09.19.62–02.24.64	discharged for commission as first lieutenant, 25th Infantry, United States Colored Troops; buried at Baptist/Methodist Evergreen Cemetery, Plainfield
John E. Price		sergeant	K 9th NJ Infantry	10.15.61–12.07.64	
		promoted first sergeant		09.01.64	Rahway resident
Joseph H. Price	(d. 11.18.64)	private	B 3rd NJ Infantry	04.27.61–07.29.61	died at Dutch Gap, VA; buried in Rahway Cemetery; $300 UC bounty
William W. Provost	(1841–05.11.1900)	private	unassigned 134th NY Infantry	01.02.64–06.10.65	recruit; buried in Section Lawncrest B, Soldiers Plot 88, Grave 30, Evergreen Cemetery, Hillside

Name	Birth-Death	Rank	Company/Regiment	In/Out	Miscellaneous
Tunis Pur/Peer	(d. 08.20.64)	private	K 9th NJ Infantry	08.14.62–08.20.64	recruit; died of diarrhea at Andersonville, GA; buried in grave 6298, National Cemetery, Andersonville, GA
James Quinn	(d. 04.25.82)	private	H 8th NJ Infantry	08.03.64–07.17.65	substitute
			C 9th NJ Infantry 03.20.65, recruit		
			K 9th NJ Infantry	09.29.64–12.18.64	substitute; buried in Section D, Plot 160, Rahway Cemetery
Aaron F. Randolph	(d. 03.09.63)	private	H 30th NJ Infantry	09.17.62–03.09.63	died of fever at hospital near Belle Plains, VA; Elizabeth resident
Charles H. Randolph	(1844–06.02.1918)	sergeant	H 30th NJ Infantry	09.17.62–06.27.63	
		promoted corporal		08.30.62	
		sergeant		05.10.63	
		private	A 4th NJ Infantry	03.24.65–07.09.65	substitute; buried in Division 8, Section A, Plot 7-Day, Grave 15, Hillside Cemetery, Scotch Plains
George W. Randolph	(1845–04.05.1916)	private	D PA 77th Infantry	02.22.64–10.18.65	Plainfield; buried in Division 8, Section A, Soldier Plot, Grave 23, Hillside Cemetery, Scotch Plains
James F. Randolph	(1839–04.11.1907)	private	D 70th NY Infantry	06.21.61–03.18.62	discharged for disability at Camp Farnum, MD; Linden resident; buried at Baptist/Methodist Evergreen Cemetery, Plainfield
Joseph C. Randolph	(b. 1843)	private	H 30th NJ Infantry	09.17.62–06.27.63	Plainfield hometown; $100 UC bounty

Name	Birth-Death	Rank	Company/Regiment	In/Out	Miscellaneous
William B. Randolph	(1845–06.20.80)	private	12th NY light Artillery	01.4.65–06.15.65	
			B NJ 1st Light Artillery		
			Battery C U.S. Army 5th Light Artillery		buried in Section C, Lot 91, Rahway Cemetery
William H. Randolph	(1831–03.8.1909)	private	K 6th NJ Infantry	08.29.61–10.12.64	
			transferred into G 8th NJ Infantry	10.12.64–07.17.65	
		promoted corporal		10.04.64	
		sergeant		12.01.64	
		reduced to private at discharge			Rahway hometown; buried in Section E, Plot 294, Rahway Cemetery
John H. Ray	(1840–1874)	sergeant	I 43rd New York Infantry		buried at Evergreen Cemetery, Hillside; $300 UC bounty
David Reed	(1845–12.12.65)	private	K 9th NJ Infantry	02.24.65–07.12.65	recruit
			transferred, G 9th NJ Infantry		
		promoted corporal		06.15.65	mulatto; Elizabeth resident; died of chronic bronchitis at Louveture Hospital, Alexandria, VA; buried in Section B, Alexandria National Cemetery, VA
Samuel W. Reese	(d. 05.28.1913)	private	G 1st Pennsylvania Cavalry		Plainfield resident
John W. Ricketts		private	K 9th NJ Infantry	08.31.64–06.14.65	recruit; discharged at Greensboro, NC

Name	Birth-Death	Rank	Company/Regiment	In/Out	Miscellaneous
James Riley	(1843–11.10.64)	private	G 9th NJ Infantry	10.01.64–05.22.65	substitute; Rahway resident; mulatto; died of diarrhea while a prisoner of war in Salisbury Prison, NC; buried at Salisbury National Cemetery, NC
Michael Riley	(d. 06.24.65)	private	Battery B, 1st NJ Artillery	09.21.64–06.16.65	recruit; Linden resident
Samuel L. Roberts	(1822–1881)	private	K 15th NJ Infantry	08.25.62–08.12.63	
		private	C 10th NJ Infantry	11.20.63–02.26.64	
			I 2nd NJ Infantry	02.26.64–07.11.65	Union resident; buried at Mt. Laurel, Burlington County; $300 UC bounty
John B. Robinson	(d. 08.20.1919)	private	K 10th United States Cavalry		buried in Section B, Grave 241, Rahway Cemetery
John Howard Robinson	(1842–10.22.64)	private	G 7th NJ Infantry	09.21.61–10.07.64	died at Camp William Penn, Philadelphia, PA; Linden; buried at Cypress Hill Cemetery, Brooklyn, NY
Joseph C. Robinson	(1840–10.29.78)	corporal	K 106th NY Infantry	08.27.62–07.04.65	
		promoted sergeant		11.01.62	
		second lieutenant	Company C	01.21.63	
		first lieutenant		03.15.63	
		captain	Company E	03.01.65	buried in Section M, Grave 88, Rahway Cemetery

Name	Birth-Death	Rank	Company/Regiment	In/Out	Miscellaneous
Rutus L. Robinson	(1828–10.13.1916)	private	D 121st NY Infantry	08.23.62–05.27.65	discharged for severe wound in right forearm, amputated on 08.20.65; wounded at Petersburg, VA, on 04.02.65; buried in Section C, Row 1, Block 127, Grave 3, Fairview Cemetery, Westfield
Samuel L. Robinson	(1843–02.25.83)	private	E 11th NJ Infantry	08.18.62–06.21.65	buried in Section M, Grave 177, Rahway Cemetery
Thomas Peter Robinson	(1844–05.20.1906)	private	H 6th NJ Infantry	05.23.64–07.19.64	
			A 40th NJ Infantry	10.11.64–10.25.64	wounded at Fort Wagner, SC, on 07.18.63; occupation: farmer; buried Section F, Soldiers Plot, Hazelwood Cemetery, Rahway
John K. Roll	(1832–1881)	private	G 52nd NY Infantry	09.01.63–09.17.64	
			transferred to C 52nd NY Infantry	09.17.64–06.01.65	Linden hometown
Elihu H. Ropes	(1845–1898)	private	11th NY Independent Battery	08.18.62–06.13.65	promoted 011.02.64; resigned after reduction in army rank; Elizabeth born; buried at Baptist/Methodist Evergreen Cemetery, Plainfield
Henry T. Rose	(b. 1823)	private	E 14th NJ Infantry	08.26.62–06.18.65	born in St. Johns, New Brunswick; Linden hometown
Royal H. Rose		second lieutenant	H 30th NJ Infantry	04.05.63–06.27.63	Linden hometown; $100 UC bounty, 08.27.62

Name	Birth-Death	Rank	Company/Regiment	In/Out	Miscellaneous
James Ross	(d. 11.23.1921)	private	B 15th NJ Infantry	02.22.65–07.11.65	drafted
			transferred into I 2nd NJ Infantry		buried in Morningside Section-Row 2, Block 607, Grave 2, Fairview Cemetery, Westfield
Joseph Ross	(d. 10.16.1900)	hospital steward	U.S. Army Infantry		buried in Colored Map 4 Division, Row-4 Adult, Grave A. Evergreen Cemetery, Hillside
Augustus Rue		private	H 11th NJ Infantry		wounded at the Battle of Fredericksburg, VA; buried at Fairview Cemetery, Westfield; $300 UC bounty, 1863
John R.T. Ryan	(d. 08.23.64)	private	A 4th NJ Infantry	02.13.64–07.09.85	recruit; Linden resident; died in Philadelphia; buried in Section C, Grave 5, Gettysburg Cemetery, PA
Elcazer Ryno	(d. 12.05.98)	private	I 2nd District of Columbia Volunteers	02.63–1.64	buried in Section C, Plot 83, Rahway Cemetery
John Ryno	(1835–06.03.64)	corporal	E 14th NJ Infantry	08.26.62–06.03.64	
		reduced to private		03.15.63	taken prisoner at Harpers Ferry, VA, 09.15.62; paroled 09.16.62; wounded in action at Cold Harbor, VA, on 06.01.64; died en route from battlefield at Cold Harbor to White House Landing, VA
William Ryno	(1832–05.09.1901)	private	D 2nd NJ Infantry	01.27.64–06.30.65	recruit; discharged for wounds received in action; occupation: blacksmith, carpenter; buried in Section F, Soldiers Plot, Hazelwood Cemetery, Rahway

Name	Birth-Death	Rank	Company/Regiment	In/Out	Miscellaneous
James Sales	(b. 1838)	private	C 88th Ohio Infantry	10.15.62–03.07.63	discharged for disability
			C 69th Ohio Infantry	03.23.64–07.17.65	$300 Bounty 1st Ward, Elizabeth bounty
Jonathan B. Sanders	(b. 1839)	private	F 50th Pennsylvania Infantry	03.11.65–07.30.65	substitute
		promoted corporal		07.01.65	Rahway hometown
Henry Sax	(1831–1902)	private	H 5th NJ Infantry	08.23.61–09.07.64	Rahway hometown; occupation: laborer; buried at Rahway Cemetery
John Henry Schenck	(b. 1834)	private	D 70th NY Infantry	06.26.61–07.01.64	prisoner of war at Chancellorsville, VA, 05.03.63; slightly wounded at Battle of Brandy Station, VA; Rahway resident
Henry F. Schenk	(b. 1840)	private	E 9th NJ Infantry, substitute	04.08.65–07.12.65	Plainfield resident
Peter Schenk		private	E 15th NJ Infantry	08.25.62–06.22.65	Plainfield
Charles H. Scott	(1842–04.30.65)	private	I 24th NJ Infantry	09.16.62–06.29.63	
			C 33rd NJ Infantry	12.09.63–07.17.65	Linden; died of chronic diarrhea Ward Hospital, Newark; $300 UC bounty
William A. Scott	(1833–1899)	private	A 1st NJ Infantry	05.21.61–06.04.62	discharged for disability at Philadelphia; born in West Indies; Elizabeth hometown

Name	Birth-Death	Rank	Company/Regiment	In/Out	Miscellaneous
John W. Simmonds	(1840–08.19.64)	private	K 9th NJ Infantry	01.05.64–08.09.64	recruit; taken prisoner at Drury's Bluff, VA, 05.16.64; died of diarrhea in rebel prison at Andersonville, GA; Elizabeth hometown; buried in grave 5,087, Andersonville Cemetery, GA; removed to Section E-Green, Evergreen Cemetery, Hillside
Thomas S. Simmons	(1841–1902)	private	B 84th PA Infantry	12.11.61–09.01.62	
		corporal	B 24th NJ Infantry	09.01.62–02.06.63	
		promoted corporal		08.30.62	
		sergeant		02.06.63	wounded and taken prisoner of war at Chancellorsville, VA, on 05.03.63; Elizabeth resident
William H. Simms	(b. 1841)	private	L 1st Michigan Engineers	12.31.63–06.12.65	born in Canada; occupation: waiter
Edward M. Slater	(1842–02.14.99)	corporal	C 14th NJ Infantry	08.26.62–11.01.63	
		reduced to private	transferred to U.S. Army Signal Corps	11.01.63–07.10.65	former slave; Rahway resident; buried in Section K, Plot 715 Rahway Cemetery
Samuel Slater		sergeant	H 30th NJ Infantry	09.17.62–06.27.63	Linden resident; $100 UC bounty, 09.02.62

Name	Birth-Death	Rank	Company/Regiment	In/Out	Miscellaneous
George F. Smith	(b. 1832)	private	G 9th NJ Infantry	08.15.62–06.14.65	recruit
			temporarily attached to C 1st Rhode Island Artillery		
		promoted corporal		08.15.64–04.07.65	
		sergeant		04.07.65–07.08.65	buried at Evergreen Cemetery, Hillside
James Smith	(1846–1879)	private	K 9th NJ Infantry	12.27.64–07.12.65	substitute; Elizabeth resident
John W.B. Smith	(1821–11.14.63)	private	B 11th NJ Infantry	07.16.62–09.63	
			transferred to Veteran Reserve Corps		died at USA Hospital, Portsmouth Grove, RI; mulatto; born in Springfield; $300 UC bounty, 03.27.63
Theodore F. Smith		private		10.02.61–10.01.64	
			transferred to Company C, 10.01.64; reenlisted 10.04.64		Rahway resident
William M. Smith	(d. 10.10.64)	musician	G 9th NJ Infantry	09.30.61–10.10.64	
		promoted corporal		03.30.63	died of yellow fever at hospital, Morehead City, NC

Name	Birth-Death	Rank	Company/Regiment	In/Out	Miscellaneous
Henry C. Stanford	(b. 1843)	corporal	A 101st NY Infantry	09.18.61–12.24.62	
			transferred into B 37th NY Infantry		
		reduced to private		12.24.62	buried at Evergreen Cemetery, Hillside
Joseph S. Stansbury		private	G 1st NJ Infantry	05.16.61–11.29.62	discharged at White Oak Church, VA, for wounds received in action at Gaines Farm, VA; Rahway resident
John E. Stewart	(1840–10.10.1925)	private	D 44th NY Infantry	09.13.61–11.10.63	
		promoted corporal		03.15.63	buried in grave 6-A-3-7 Hillside Cemetery, Scotch Plains
William Scott Stewart	(1842–1900)	commissioned assistant surgeon	83rd Pennsylvania Infantry	05.22.63–09.20.64	
		assistant surgeon	123rd PA Infantry		
		assistant surgeon		03.25.63–05.13.63	
		corporal	D 40th NJ Infantry	01.27.65–07.08.65	mulatto, born in Ireland; buried at Baptist/Methodist Evergreen Cemetery, Plainfield
Charles R. Still	(1834–1905)	private	K 82nd NY Infantry	05.21.61–01.22.63	discharged for disability at Fort Monroe, VA; born in Elizabethtown; buried at Evergreen Cemetery, Hillside
Aaron W. Sutton	(d. 07.16.96)	private	B 11th NJ Infantry	06.10.62–01.15.63	discharged at Convalescent Camp, Alexandria, VA; buried in Section 9, Plot 4, Baptist/Methodist Evergreen Cemetery, Plainfield

Name	Birth-Death	Rank	Company/Regiment	In/Out	Miscellaneous
Benjamin Sutton	(1837–1907)	corporal	H 67th NY Infantry	06.24.61–07.04.64	
		promoted sergeant		07.19.62	
		reduced to private		12.09.62	buried in Division 5, Section C, Row 7 and 8, Grave 34, Hillside Cemetery, Scotch Plains
Charles Sutton	(1848–1879)	private	D 14th NJ Infantry	08.26.62–06.18.65	
		promoted captain		06.25.64	Elizabeth hometown
Charles H. Taylor	(1843–05.5.62)	private	I 8th NJ Infantry	11.09.61–05.05.62	killed in action at Williamsburg, VA; mulatto; occupation: cook and steward; Rahway hometown
Cornelius P. Terhune	(d. 09.12.1918)	private	H 23rd NJ Infantry	09.23.62–06.27.63	
		corporal	E 2nd NJ Cavalry	09.16.63–03.01.65	
			transferred into Veteran Reserve Corps	03.01.65–11.25.65	buried in Section E, Plot 550, Grave 2, Evergreen Cemetery, Hillside
David B. Terhune	(d. 03.22.1920)	private	C 22nd NJ Infantry	09.22.62–06.25.63	recruit; buried in Lawncrest B, Soldiers Plot 88, Row D, Grave 4, Evergreen Cemetery, Hillside
John W. Terhune	(1833–12.26.62)	first sergeant	D 11th NJ Infantry	07.12.62–08.14.62	
			H 21st NJ Infantry	09.15.62–12.26.62	died of typhoid fever in camp near White Oak Church, VA; Elizabeth hometown
Martin Terhune	(b. 1834)	private	A 22nd NJ Infantry	09.22.62–06.25.63	recruit; Elizabeth hometown

Name	Birth-Death	Rank	Company/Regiment	In/Out	Miscellaneous
Reverend Thomas Thompson	(d. 06.23.64)	private	G 9th NJ Infantry	07.23.63–08.25.64	recruit; killed in action at Cold Harbor, VA; born in Liverpool; buried at Hazelwood Cemetery, Rahway
Randolph Thorn		corporal	H 30th NJ Infantry	09.17.62–06.27.63	
		private	Battery D, NJ 1st Regiment Light Artillery	09.13.64–06.17.65	recruit; buried at Baptist/Methodist Evergreen Cemetery, Plainfield
George Thornton		private	F 2nd Regiment Cavalry	09.06.64–05.15.65	recruit; discharged at Memphis, TN; Linden
Samuel M. Till	(1835–02.11.65)	private	K 13th NJ Infantry	08.30.64–02.11.65	recruit; died of epilepsy at Field Hospital, Duncan's Brigade, SC; buried at Baptist/Methodist Evergreen Cemetery, Plainfield
Henry C. Tilton	(1838–10.01.64)	first lieutenant	B 11th NJ Infantry	11.24.63–08.01.64	resigned on account of disability
		reduced to private		10.31.63	died at Morris Island, SC
Nathan C. Tooker	(1831–1904)	sergeant	A 2nd NJ infantry	05.22.61–06.21.64	
		promoted first sergeant		07.28.61	
		reduced to private		12.01.62	buried at Evergreen Cemetery, Hillside
John B. Turner	(1844–1882)	private	I 2nd District of Columbia Volunteers	02.29.64–09.12.65	occupation: potter/carpenter; Rahway hometown; buried at Rahway Cemetery

Name	Birth-Death	Rank	Company/Regiment	In/Out	Miscellaneous
Samuel Turner		private	B 13th NJ Infantry	11.30.63–06.08.65	
			transferred into unassigned 33rd NJ Infantry		
		promoted corporal		05.01.65	
		reduced to private	I 8th NJ Infantry	09.07.64–06.04.65	substitute; Cranford resident
George Tuttle	(b. 1836)	corporal	E 27th NJ Infantry	09.04.62–07.02.63	
		promoted corporal		03.01.63	occupation: mariner; Elizabeth born
Eugene van Campen	(1840–1905)	private	A 1st New York Heavy Artillery		Plainfield hometown; buried at Hillside Cemetery, Scotch Plains
Jessie Vanderhoven	(1817–1901)	private	C 30th NJ Infantry	09.17.62–06.27.63	
			Battery D, 1st Regiment Light Artillery	09.30.64–06.17.65	recruit; buried at Hazelwood Cemetery, Rahway
John H. Vanderveer	(1838–1913)	captain	E 15th NJ Infantry	08.25.62–07.19.64	resigned for wounds
		promoted commanding captain		12.26.62–08.24.65	buried at Fairview Cemetery, Westfield
Peter Vanderveer	(b. 1842)	sergeant	K 70th NY Infantry	06.21.61–03.20.62	discharged for disability
		reduced to private	A 38th NJ Infantry	09.22.64–06.30.65	occupation: farmer; Elizabeth resident

Name	Birth-Death	Rank	Company/Regiment	In/Out	Miscellaneous
William H. Vanderveer	(b. 1843)	private	F 29th NJ Infantry	09.1.62– 06.30.63	Plainfield born
James O. van Fleet			G 32nd NY Infantry		
			F 9th NJ Infantry	10.15.61– 11.17.62	occupation: livery; Plainfield hometown
John W. van Horn	(1837–03.11.1901)	private	A 14th NJ Infantry	08.02.62– 06.08.65	
		private	B 6th NJ Infantry	09.10.61– 09.15.62	discharged at U.S. Army General Hospital, Philadelphia, PA; buried at Hillside Cemetery, Scotch Plains
William H. van Horn	(d. 08.27.62)	private	B 104th Pennsylvania Cavalry		
		private	A 2nd NJ Infantry	05.04.61– 08.27.62	killed in action at Manassas, VA
James C. van Houten	(b. 1842)		C 14th NJ Infantry	08.26.62– 01.01.65	
			transferred to Veteran Reserve Corps	01.01.65– 06.29.65	
		discharged as corporal			Elizabeth hometown; $100 UC bounty
John J. van Houten	(1837–1882)	corporal	A 22nd NJ Infantry	09.01.62– 06.25.63	Elizabeth hometown; buried in Division B, Section C, Grave 30, Fredericksburg Cemetery, VA
William Vannaman		private	C 30th NJ Infantry	09.06.64– 06.25.65	recruit; discharged at Cliffburne U.S. Army General Hospital, Washington, D.C., with disability
David H. van Pelt	(b. 1846)	private	B 11th NJ Infantry	07.21.62– 06.06.65	occupation: oysterman; Elizabeth resident; buried at Evergreen Cemetery, Hillside

Name	Birth-Death	Rank	Company/Regiment	In/Out	Miscellaneous
George van Pelt	(1845–1918)	private	E 4th NY Heavy Artillery	12.63–06.65	occupation: oysterman; Elizabeth resident; buried at Evergreen Cemetery, Hillside
Jacob D. van Pelt	(d. 07.09.63)	private	B 11th NJ Infantry	07.14.62–07.09.63	died at USA General Hospital, Baltimore, MD, of wounds received in action at Gettysburg, PA; occupation: boatman; Elizabeth resident; buried A-83, NY Plot, Gettysburg National Cemetery, Gettysburg, PA
Jeremiah van Pelt		private	B 11th NJ Infantry	08.08.62–03.05.63	discharged at USA Hospital, Portsmouth Grove, RI, with disability; Elizabeth hometown; occupation: oysterman; buried at Evergreen Cemetery, Hillside
John W. van Pelt	(b. 1843)	quartermaster	D 36th Illinois Infantry	09.23.61–09.22.64	
		promoted quartermaster		03.03.62	buried at Evergreen Cemetery, Hillside
John van Riper	(b. 1845)	private	G 27th NJ Infantry	09.03.62–07.02.63	discharged for disability at Summit House Hospital, Philadelphia, PA; occupation: waiter; Linden resident
Albert van Sickles	(1822–1880)	private	E 14th NJ Infantry	08.08.62–08.31.63	discharged at Jarvis, U.S. Army General Hospital, Baltimore, MD; occupation: teamster; Linden resident; $100 UC bounty
Nathan P. Vermeule	(d. 03.09.63)	private	H 30th NJ Infantry	09.17.62–03.09.63	died of disease; Plainfield resident

Name	Birth-Death	Rank	Company/Regiment	In/Out	Miscellaneous
Charles A. Voorhees		corporal	B 11th NJ Infantry	08.15.62–05.03.63	discharged at USA General Hospital, Newark, for wounds received in action at Gettysburg, PA; $100 UC bounty
Edmund A. Voorhees		private	C 14th NJ Infantry	08.12.62–04.19.64	
			transferred to U.S. Navy	04.19.64	Elizabeth resident
Henry Voorhees		wagoner	C 9th NJ Infantry	01.18.64–07.12.65	recruit
Jeremiah Voorhees	(1828–1880)	private	B 11th NJ Infantry	08.08.62–03.05.63	discharged for disability at USA Hospital, Portsmouth Grove, RI; occupation: laborer; buried at Rahway Cemetery
Jeremiah F. Voorhees	(1841–06.11.62)	private	A NY 9th NY Infantry	05.04.61–06.11.62	wounded at River Bridge, NC, 04.19.1862; died at Lebanon, NJ
John C. Voorhees	(d. 07.20.64)	private	B 11th NJ Infantry	08.16.62–06.06.65	
		promoted corporal		10.30.64	
		sergeant		12.16.64	
Nicholas H. Voorhis	(b. 1843)	private	A 22nd NJ Infantry	09.22.62–02.28.63	recruit
Thomas H. Walker	(1838–1903)	private	C 14th NJ Infantry	08.20.62–06.24.65	discharged at USA Hospital, Newark, for wounds received in action at Monocacy, MD, 07.09.64; born in Elizabeth; buried at Evergreen Cemetery, Hillside
John Wallace	(b. 1837)	private	K 13th NJ Infantry	08.25.62–06.08.65	mulatto; Linden resident
Charles W. Ward	(b. 1838)	wagoner	G 9th NJ Infantry	09.30.61–07.12.65	reenlisted 01.18.64; Rahway resident

Name	Birth-Death	Rank	Company/Regiment	In/Out	Miscellaneous
John Ward	(1839–07.22.1915)	private	K 9th NJ Infantry	10.15.61–08.18.65	
		private	I 14th NJ Infantry	04.17.63–06.18.65	discharged at USA General Hospital, Newark, for wounds received in action; buried in nonsectarian cemetery, Rosedale Cemetery, Linden
Thomas Ward		private	E 14th NJ Infantry	08.20.62–06.28.65	Linden resident
William Ward	(1843–1896)	private	G 9th NJ Infantry	10.30.61–07.12.65	
		promoted corporal		07.01.63	reenlisted 11.25.63
		reduced to private		02.01.65	
		private	Battery E, First Regiment NJ Light Artillery	02.28.65–07.11.65	recruit; wounded at Walthall, VA, 05.06.64; buried at Hazelwood Cemetery, Rahway
George Watson	(b. 1836)	private	K 3rd NJ Infantry	07.08.61–09.20.62	recruit; discharged at Fort McHenry, MD, with disability; Linden resident
Thomas F. Watson	(1844–09.22.64)	private	I 14th NJ Infantry	08.26.62–03.31.64	Linden resident; buried at Andersonville Cemetery, GA
Charles White	(b. 1841)	private	K 9th New York State Militia	02.27.64–07.08.65	Linden resident
George A. White	(1839–03.03.95)	private	G 14th NJ Infantry	08.26.62–04.19.64	buried in Section M, Grave 229, Rahway Cemetery

Name	Birth-Death	Rank	Company/Regiment	In/Out	Miscellaneous
James H. White	(1840–12.27.1929)	private	H 35th NJ Infantry	09.24.63–07.20.65	
		promoted corporal		03.08.64	
		reduced to private		12.21.64; promoted 01.01.65	buried at Fairview Cemetery, Westfield
Louis F. White	(1844–1903)	private	H 14th NY Heavy Artillery	10.09.64–06.30.65	buried at Rahway Cemetery
George W. Whitehead		private	G 8th NJ Infantry	09.23.64–01.30.65	recruit; Elizabeth hometown; buried at Evergreen Cemetery, Hillside
James H. Whitehead		private	K 13th NJ Infantry	08.25.62–06.08.65	$300 Rahway bounty, 1863
George W. Whitney	(1834–04.29.65)		1st Sharpshooters, 27th Michigan Infantry	03.01.64–05.23.65	
		corporal	G 9th NJ Infantry	04.10.65–07.12.65	recruit
			transferred from Company K		Elizabeth resident
Charles A. Williams	(b. 1843)	private	K 9th NJ Infantry	03.07.62–02.16.65	recruit; reenlisted 03.11.64; wounded in arm at Drury's Bluff 05.16.64; discharged at USA Hospital, Newark, NJ; disability; Linden resident
Frederick L. Williams		private	K 38th NJ Infantry	09.6.64–06.30.65	
			G 2nd Regiment District of Columbia Volunteers	02.15.65–09.12.65	recruit; discharged at Alexandria, VA; Linden resident
James H. Williams	(1831–04.08.94)	private	G 9th NJ Infantry	02.18.64–07.19.65	recruit; Elizabeth hometown; buried at Evergreen Cemetery, Hillside

Name	Birth-Death	Rank	Company/Regiment	In/Out	Miscellaneous
Robert S. Williams	(d. 07.13.1918)	private	K 9th NJ Infantry	10.15.61–12.07.64	
		promoted corporal		02.09.62	
		sergeant		06.03.63	wounded in arm at Drury's Bluff, VA 05.16.64; Union resident; buried at Evergreen Cemetery, Hillside
William H. Williams	(1836–1911)	private	A 9th NJ Infantry	09.28.64–05.29.65	substitute; captured at Drury's Bluff, VA, 05.16.64; discharged 07.12.65; mulatto; born in England; Plainfield; buried at nonsectarian cemetery, Linden
William H. Wills		private	B 24th NJ Infantry	09.16.62–06.29.63	
		promoted corporal		01.20.63	
		sergeant		03.21.63	Elizabeth resident
Henry Wilson	(1814–10.10.62)	private	A 2nd NJ Infantry	04.27.61–07.01.62	wounded and taken prisoner in action at Malvern Hill, VA; exchanged; died on board transport en route to regiment; buried at Evergreen Cemetery, Hillside
Henry F. Wilson	(1844–11.27.63)	private	C 14th NJ Infantry	08.16.62–11.27.63	killed in action at Locust Grove, VA; Elizabeth; buried at Evergreen Cemetery, Hillside
James Wilson	(1828–1895)	private	H 5th NJ Infantry	08.23.61–05.06.62	slave prior to 04.19.61; Elizabeth, hometown; buried at Evergreen Cemetery, Hillside
Alfred L. Winans		private	D 11th NJ Infantry	08.05.62–12.11.63	recruit; discharged at USA Hospital, Newark, NJ, with disability; Linden; $300 UC bounty

Name	Birth-Death	Rank	Company/Regiment	In/Out	Miscellaneous
Theodore Winans		private	B 13th NJ Infantry	01.26.65–06.08.65	$300 3rd Ward, Elizabeth bounty
Amos T. Wood	(1843–03.13.81)	corporal	F 29th NJ Infantry	09.20.62–07.06.63	buried in Section M, Grave 155, Rahway Cemetery; $300 UC bounty
Henry Wood	(1839–1909)	private	I 10th NJ Infantry	03.23.64–05.02.64	occupation: lumber; Elizabeth hometown; buried at Rosehill Cemetery, Linden
Charles Woods	(d. 05.09.64)	private	K 3rd NJ Infantry	09.13.62–05.09.64	recruit; killed in action at Spotsylvania, VA; Rahway hometown
Edward Wright	(1844–1879)	private	H 21st NJ Infantry	09.15.62–06.13.63	recruit
		promoted corporal		02.14.63	severely wounded in right leg at Salem Heights, VA, 05.03.63; discharged for wounds; $250 UC bounty, 01.09.63
James Wright	(1819–1879)	cook	C 3rd NJ Cavalry	12.15.63–02.22.64	Elizabeth resident; buried at Evergreen Cemetery, Hillside
William Wright	(1840–08.21.84)	private	5th NY Artillery	08.18.62–06.22.65	
		promoted artificer		11.01.62	buried in Section M, Grave 783, Rahway Cemetery
Albert Voorhees Wyckoff	(1844–06.02.64)	corporal	E 15th NJ Infantry	08.25.62–06.02.64	died of wounds received in action at Cold Harbor, VA
Benjamin Wyckoff		private	A 31st NJ Infantry	09.17.62–06.24.63	Plainfield resident; buried in Section 3, Plot 300, Baptist/Methodist Evergreen Cemetery, Plainfield

Name	Birth-Death	Rank	Company/Regiment	In/Out	Miscellaneous
Charles B. Wyckoff	(1842–08.26.76)	second lieutenant	H 48th NY Infantry	11.20.63–03.07.64	
		promoted second lieutenant	A 48th NY Infantry	07.10.63	buried in Strangers Section, Rahway Cemetery
Hiram G. Wyckoff		private	E 124th Illinois Infantry	08.10.62–04.23.63	Elizabeth hometown
Thomas Wyckoff	(b. 1844)	second lieutenant	G 3rd Michigan Infantry	09.07.64–05.25.66	
		promoted second lieutenant		11.28.65	discharged with disability; Plainfield resident
Jacob H. Zabriskie	(1840–11.22.82)	first sergeant	D 144th NY Infantry	09.27.62–09.01.63	
		promoted first sergeant		03.05.63	mulatto; Linden resident

Notes

Preface

1. Wilson, *The Black Phalanx*.

1. Black Life in Union County: 1857–66

2. *U.S. Census Office, 8th Census, 1860*. Trenton, NJ: Phillips and Boswell, 1862.
3. *Liberator*, April 12, 1834.
4. Bishop Campbell, "The War and Its Issues," *Christian Recorder*, June 3, 1865.
5. Private Walter G. Dunn to Emma Randolph, October 30, 1864, in Bailey and Cottom, *After Chancellorsville*.
6. *Christian Recorder*, "Colored Men to Vote," August 25, 1866.

2. Union County Regiments, Recruitment and Enlistments

7. Wilson, *The Black Phalanx*, 179–80.
8. A Registry of the Volunteers that Received the Bounty from Union County, New Jersey, New Jersey Civil War Document, Volume 1, August

12–November 12, 1862, 39. Special Collections and University Archives of Rutgers University.

3. United States Colored Troops (USCT): 1862–66

9. Wilson, *The Black Phalanx*, 175.
10. *Christian Recorder*, May 5, 1866.
11. *Chicago Defender*, August 7, 1985.

4. Sailors: United States Navy and Marine Corps

12. Joseph P. Reider, "Black Men in Navy Blue During the Civil War, Part 2," *Prologue Magazine* 33, no 3 (Fall 2001).

5. Rahway Contributions to the War Effort

13. Walker, *The Civil War*.
14. Minutes of a Meeting of the Brigade Board, Union County, New Jersey. New Jersey Civil War Document, March 27, 1861, 2. Special Collections and University Archives of Rutgers University.
15. Stephen T. Foster, *U.S. Zouave Cadets*, Atlas Editions, USA, 1993.
16. Minutes of the Rahway City Council, April 17, 1865. Merchants & Drovers Tavern Museum Association, Rahway, New Jersey. 2005.

Bibliography

Bailey, Judith A., and Robert I. Cottom, eds. *After Chancellorsville, Letters from the Heart.* Baltimore: Maryland Historical Society, 1998.

Bethel, Leonard L., and Frederick A. Johnson, eds. *Plainfield's African-American: From Northern Slavery to Church Freedom.* Lanham, NY: University Press of America, 1998.

Buckley, Gail. *American Patriots: The Story of Blacks in the Military from the Revolution to Desert Storm.* New York: Random House Trade Paperbacks, 2001.

The City of Elizabeth New Jersey Illustrated, Showing its Leading Characteristics: Its Attractions as a Place of Residence, and Its Unsurpassed Advantages as a Location for Manufacturing Industries. Elizabeth, NJ: *Elizabeth Daily Journal*, 1889.

Clayton, W. Woodford, ed. *History of Union and Middlesex Counties, New Jersey.* Philadelphia, PA: Everts and Peck, 1882.

Crew, Spencer. *Black Life in Secondary Cities: A Comparative Analysis of the Black Communities of Camden and Elizabeth, NJ 1860–1920.* New York and London: Garland Publishing, 1993.

Cunningham, Barbara, ed. *The New Jersey Ethnic Experience.* Union City, NJ: Wm. H. Wise & Co., 1977.

Drake, Captain J. Madison. *The History of the Ninth New Jersey Veteran Vols.* Elizabeth, NJ: Journal Printing House, 74 Broad St., 1889.

Edgar, George P. *History of the Second Presbyterian Church of Rahway, N.J., 1849–1887.* Rahway, NJ: W.L. Mershon & Co., 1887.

Everts, Hermann. *A Complete and Comprehensive History of the 9th Regiment New Jersey Vols. Infantry: From its First Organization to Its Final Muster Out.* Newark, NJ: A. Stephen Holbrook, printer, 1865.

Foster, John. *New Jersey and the Rebellion: History of the Services of the Troops and People of New Jersey in Aid of the Union Cause.* Newark, NJ: 1868.

Gillette, William. *Jersey Blue: Civil War Politics in New Jersey, 1854–1865.* New Brunswick, NJ: Rutgers University Press, 1994.

Hodges, Graham Russell. *Root & Branch: African Americans in New York & East Jersey, 1613–1863.* Chapel Hill and London: University of North Carolina Press, 1999.

Honeyman, A. van Doren, editor in chief. *History of Union County New Jersey: 1664–1923, Vol. I.* New York and Chicago: Lewis Historical Publishing, 1923.

Lee, Francis Bazley. *New Jersey as a Colony and a State: One of the Original Thirteen, Vol. IV.* New York: Publishing Society of New Jersey, 1902.

McPherson, James M. *The Negro's Civil War: How American Blacks Felt and Acted During the War for the Union.* New York: Vintage Books, a Division of Random House, Inc., 2003.

Olsen, Bernard A., ed. *Upon the Tented Field.* Red Bank, NJ: Historic Projects, Inc., 1993.

Philadelphia (Pennsylvania) Supervisory Committee for Recruiting Colored Regiments. *Free Military School for Commands of Colored Troops.* N.p.: 1864.

Ricord, F.W., ed. *History of Union County New Jersey.* Newark, NJ: East Jersey History Company, 1897.

Sinclair, Donald A. *A Bibliography: The Civil War and New Jersey.* New Brunswick: Published by the Friends of the Rutgers University Library for the New Jersey Civil War Centennial Commission, 1968.

———. *A Guide to New Jersey and Other Civil War Manuscripts in the Special Collections and University Archives of Rutgers University /compiled by Donald Arleigh Sinclair.* New Brunswick, NJ: Special Collections and University Archives, Anno, 2003.

Turner, Jean-Rae. *Once Upon A Time, A Collection of Local Historical Columns.* Compiled by Richard T. Koles. Cranford, NJ: Union County Historical Society, 2008.

Walker, David M. *The Civil War on the Battlefield and the Home Front.* Rahway, NJ: Merchants and Drovers Tavern Museum Association, 2005.

Wilson, Joseph T. *The Black Phalanx: A History of the Negro Soldiers of the United States in the Wars of 1775–1812, 1861–'65.* Hartford, CT: American Publishing Company, 1888.

About the Author

Ethel M. Washington is the history programs coordinator at the Union County Office of Cultural & Heritage Affairs. Ms. Washington established the African American Design Archive at the Cooper-Hewitt National Design Museum, Smithsonian Institution, where she worked prior to assuming her current position. She is a founding board member and vice chair of the New Jersey Black Cultural & Heritage Foundation, Inc. She is a contributor to the *Encyclopedia New Jersey and Union County 150th Anniversary Magazine* and authored *Union County Black Americans* and the award-winning *African American Design Archive* brochure. She is the recipient of numerous awards and honors, including induction into the Linden Historical Society's Hall of Fame, Union County Women of Excellence Award and Luminous Award from the Raritan Valley Chapter of Links, Inc. She is a graduate of Central State University of Ohio and holds two master's degrees from Columbia University. She pursued doctoral studies at Rutgers University where she also earned a certificate in museum studies.